# SAFETY
# FIRST

HEALTH
RIGHT

# SAFETY
# FIRST

## The family guide
## to accident prevention

**JAMES TYE**
**and**
**TIM CHALLIS**

*Published in association with the British Safety Council*

J. M. Dent & Sons Ltd
London   Melbourne

First published 1988

© James Tye and Tim Challis 1988

Illustrations by Stuart Dormon

This book is set in 10½/11½pt Plantin by Input Typesetting
Made in Great Britain by
Guernsey Press Co. Ltd, Guernsey, C.I. for
J.M. Dent & Sons Ltd
91, Clapham High St., London SW4 7TA

British Library Cataloguing in Publication Data

Tye, James
  Safety first: the family guide to accident prevention including first aid
  guidance.—(Healthright).
  1. Residences. Safety
  I. Title  II. Challis, Tim  III. Series
  363.1'375
  ISBN 0–460–02492–2

# CONTENTS

# ACKNOWLEDGEMENTS

Thanks to Mark Wheeler for technical information, Derek Agnew for encouragement, Morris Assaf for invaluable advice, Gary Roberts for use of his research work and Ruth Challis for her professional help. Little is original in anything, and safety as a subject would not exist without input from sources too numerous to list here. Organisations producing particularly relevant material include the Royal Society for the Prevention of Accidents (RoSPA) in Birmingham, the Consumers' Association, the Consumer Safety Unit of the Department of Trade and Industry, Age Concern, Sunderland Polytechnic (Faculty of Art and Design), the London Borough of Hammersmith and Fulham, the British Society for Social Responsibility in Science, the Health and Safety Executive, and many, many more.

In memory
of
ADRIAN YORK

# PREFACE

Since its foundation in 1957 the British Safety Council has campaigned extensively on a wide range of issues that affect people going about their daily business. We believe that this has given us a thorough understanding both of the nature of the safety problems facing people, and of the solutions that best suit their varying situations.

From many points of view, this accumulated experience would appear to lead to depressing conclusions. Despite advances in systems and technology, accident figures are still high, and in some areas they are still rising. Indeed, cynics might (and sometimes do) argue that a certain number of people are always going to suffer accidents, and that safety as a subject and ideal is therefore something that can be taken too far.

The Safety Council does not hold this view. Human error is the cause of the vast majority of accidents at work and in the home; if the element of error, usually itself the product of ignorance, can be eliminated, then so is the likelihood of an accident. This will only happen when people learn to 'think' safety, and work out possible risks and precautions for themselves.

At work, people can be protected by a number of different organisations: their safety reps, their union and the Health and Safety Executive for a start. But at home they have to look after their own welfare.

The dangers that face people there are many. In the past the Safety Council managed to eradicate some, and campaign against many more: dangerous toys, children's nightwear that is highly flammable, poorly designed lifejackets, fireworks and seat belts; the list is extensive. Unfortunately it must be said that the bureaucracy of official consumer safety organisations is sometimes frustrating in the extreme. Dangerous products sometimes remain on the shelves weeks or months, some products are not removed at all, and others are only prohibited by short-term bans.

In some areas, notably that of consumer safety, recent years have seen a number of moves to improve the level of protection to which an individual should be entitled. Probably the most significant of these is the Consumer Protection Act which, from 1 October 1987, introduced an EEC Directive on Product Liability in the UK. Manufacturers are now ultimately liable for injuries or damage caused by a defective product, whether or not the fault is due to negligence, and suppliers could now face prosecution for selling 'unsafe' goods.

Part of taking the responsibility for looking after your own safety involves making every effort to unearth information about processes or materials being used. A book like this cannot hope to cover all the risks in every situation, but it can, and we hope it does, offer a comprehensive guide not just to the sorts of dangers likely to be found around the house but also to the methods and systems used for dealing with them.

Ultimately it is the individual who will have to engineer an environment in which he or she can live with both enjoyment and safety. We hope this book makes the job easier for them.

James Tye
Tim Challis

# INTRODUCTION

Health and Safety is something that is normally associated with the workplace, but in reality most of us will face our greatest risk of an accident when we are in the home, on the roads or at leisure. The dangers are many and varied, and may be very serious.

In the United Kingdom, approximately 250,000 children every year require hospital treatment following accidents involving architectural features in the home: falling down stairs, trapping fingers in doors, and other similar accidents. A further 80 might die and 1,000 become non-fatal casualties in domestic fires.

This toll extends to other areas of non-vocational activity. For instance, around 100,000 accidents occur every year in the garden, some of them fatal.

In total, the Department of Trade and Industry believes that there are as many as two million domestic accidents requiring hospital treatment annually. Add to this figure the number of people requiring medication after a domestic accident who go to their GP rather than to hospital, and the total could be as high as three million. Many of these accidents could have been avoided if simple precautions had been taken and if potential risks had been more thoroughly explored and understood.

So it is unfortunate that most people still associate safety with the more obvious manifestations of risk: aeroplane crashes, chemical disasters, fires in large public buildings, reckless driving and so on. Others may relate it to the rules and regulations imposed by safety officers at work. Safety forms part of, or should form part of, countless areas of human activity, but it is a sad fact that people rarely think of it in those terms.

This is not altogether surprising. Like many studies and

disciplines, safety has been taken out of the hands of the layman and put into the hands of the professional. This is fine when you are at your place of work where the laws of the land require your employer to provide you with certain reasonably high standards of safety. Professional safety officers will examine these standards and attempt to ensure that they are enforced. If an accident occurs, professional people will investigate it, and if it transpires that your employer has been negligent, then he will be taken to court and punished. Although the individual does share some of the responsibility for his or her own safety at work, most of the burden falls upon other people.

However, the situation changes dramatically once you finish your day at work and leave the premises to go home. Now the burden rests with you. The manner in which you use machines or processes, whether they are in the house, in the garden or in the DIY workshop, is predominantly a matter for your own discretion. For instance, while the manufacturer of an electric hammer drill intended for DIY use has a responsibility to make his product conform to a series of technical safety standards, he is obviously not going to be with you when you use it nor going to insist that the drill is properly and regularly serviced.

In the same way, the manufacturer of an electric hedge-trimmer cannot guarantee that you will not cut through your own power cable. He can recommend a series of safety systems that will, or at least may, protect you should you do so, but he cannot ensure that you adhere to them. That is up to you.

Even so, the health and safety laws that apply in the workplace are of some relevance to the promotion of safety in the home. After all, a man cutting wood on a small circular saw at work where he is, or should be, supervised and properly trained, is performing the same task as a man cutting wood on a small circular saw at home for DIY purposes.

With the exception of somebody earning a living from the work that they do at home, modified and self-imposed forms of the safety systems used in the workplace may therefore be the best way to avoid many unnecessary accidents at home.

In the case of a self-employed person working from home the laws of the workplace apply in full, and all the relevant regulations and codes of practice must be applied.

This is because the main foundation of safety at work in Britain is the Health and Safety at Work Act 1974. This law is used like an 'umbrella' under which a wide range of other acts and regulations can be gathered. Like many other similar laws, it has to define the areas to which it applies.

The Health and Safety at Work Act covers areas of employment. That is, it covers areas where people are paid for doing a job. The Act states quite specifically that it applies in full to a self-employed person as well.

For example, if you are earning a living by making wooden doors in your workshop at home you must, by law, ensure that you comply with all the regulations appropriate to woodworking machinery, your working environment, noise levels and so on. The fact that it is only your own safety at stake would make no difference as the health and safety laws are not a matter of personal choice.

If you are in this position, and earn a living from your work at home, the Health and Safety Executive will be able to offer you advice. The number of their local office will be in your telephone book.

Another reason why it is useful to have some understanding of the health and safety laws is that it explains one of the problems facing any study of home safety. Because such precise legislation is absent where safety in the home is concerned, certain facts and figures are missing. For instance, the Health and Safety at Work Act has enabled legislators to demand that accidents causing three or more days of incapacity from work must be reported.

This in turn allows us to talk authoritatively about the number of people killed or seriously injured at work every year in the United Kingdom. We can even talk about the number of people killed or injured in very specific circumstances. For example, the Health and Safety Executive's report *Deadly Maintenance* reveals that between 1980 and 1982, fifty people were killed by becoming entangled in, or trapped by, machines which they were servicing.

Likewise, their report *Transport Kills* tells us that between 1978 and 1980, fifteen people were killed by reversing fork-lift trucks at their place of work. We can then compare this statistic with that for other groups of vehicles, such as reversing refuse collection vehicles (seven fatalities) and public service vehicles (five fatalities). Once these are combined with figures such as the total number of each vehicle type in use during that period, we are in a position to make accurate comparisons of the severity and nature of risks attached to various types of reversing vehicles in the workplace.

But there is no legal requirement for you to report an accident that happens to you in the home. If you, for instance, cut your hand with a saw and require hospital treatment, you do not have to inform any government or local government body of the injury, nor of the incapacity that it caused you.

The only way that the number of home accidents can be estimated is by taking a typical sample of hospitals and recording the number of people who came to them for treatment after having received such an injury.

This has been carried out by the Department of Trade and Industry (DTI) in an annual report called *The Home Accident Surveillance System*. In this study, the DTI selects twenty hospitals throughout England and Wales that have a 24-hour Accident and Emergency service. These hospitals are asked to provide details of casualties that require treatment following a domestic accident.

From the information that the DTI receives, they can estimate with reasonable accuracy the number of home accidents throughout Great Britain for that particular twelve-month period. This is done by comparing the accident figures of the twenty selected hospitals with the percentage of the population that they cater for. The results are then extrapolated to arrive at the figure for the entire population. Of course, many other factors are taken into account, but this is essentially how the system functions.

This study, generally known as HASS, is very important in any attempt to understand home safety as it allows us to make the kinds of measurements of home safety that we can already make with safety at work, and with almost equal accuracy. We know, for example, that the frequency of accidents every year is greatest during the good-weather months of April to August.

Furthermore, we know that most of these accidents occur between 4.00 p.m. and 8.00 p.m. These may be fairly predictable observations to make – the house tends to be busiest during the early evening – but we can then progress until we are examining features such as the ages of the casualties, the cause of the accident and the severity of the injuries.

Statistics such as these will be referred to throughout the text. It is important to remember that the actual number quoted will be that for only twenty hospitals; it is the comparative risk rating that is most relevant.

For example, the 1984 HASS report shows that a total of 22,386 children were injured whilst playing in, or around, the home. Of this figure, the greatest single subtotal (4,879) was for children falling on the same level. Throughout Great Britain the actual number of children falling whilst they were playing in the home will be much greater, but this figure tells us with a high degree of accuracy that children playing are most likely to hurt themselves by falling. After falling on the same level, falling between two levels poses the greatest danger, then being struck by an object or person, then cutting or piercing, then accidental poisoning, and so on.

Without this information, identifying danger areas around the home would be largely a matter of conjecture. Because the information also gives us details of environmental and architectural features that are commonly involved in accidents, it helps to provide a structure for the safe design of living and working areas.

Other important controls on home safety are established by the British Standards Institution and by the quality approval that it offers to products on sale in the United Kingdom. These will often be referred to below.

British Standards are a series of technical quality and mechanical specifications to which manufactured products should conform. These standards are not enforceable by law, although some are moving in that direction, but they do give the consumer a fairly accurate impression of the quality of aspects of the product that he or she is buying. For instance, in the case of an electric plug, which should conform to British Standard number 1363 (BS 1363), the written standard refers to both the electrical parts of the plug and to the quality specifications of the casing. This means that the plug will not only be electrically safe, but will probably be a well-made, durable product as well.

It is also worth noting that you should try to buy British wherever possible. There have been a number of cases of foreign manufacturers attempting to reproduce both British products and their British Standard marking. This type of fake product is much less likely to occur with British manufacturers, who can be more tightly monitored.

Thus, products conforming to a British Standard should be purchased in preference to those that do not, since at least some indication of quality is given. The standard should be printed on both the product and the package; but if you are in doubt whether the article you are buying conforms to a British Standard, do not hesitate to ask your dealer to check for you.

Two other marks that are commonly printed on products conforming to a British Standard are the Kitemark and the Safety Mark. From many points of view these are more useful to the consumer, although both can only be awarded in tandem with the British Standard.

The Kitemark is a registered trade mark owned by the British Standards Institution. It can only be used by a manufacturer licensed under the Kitemark scheme, and like the British Standard it refers to particular aspects of product quality rather than just to safety. This mark, however, means that the product has been independently tested by the British Standards Institution. To qualify for a Kitemark on his product, a manufacturer must also agree to produce and maintain a quality system. This will set out the organisation, responsibilities, procedures and methods involved in manufacturing the product, and must itself conform to a British Standard (BS 5750).

The Safety Mark is not dissimilar to the Kitemark, and manufacturers have to agree to basically the same requirements as those for the Kitemark. The main difference is that the Safety Mark appears only on BSI approved products where the standards in question, or at least part of the standards in question, refer specifically to the safety of the product. This means that you know when you purchase a product that parts of it have been thoroughly tested for safety, and that it will certainly be as safe as any other product bearing just a British

Standard number, and possibly a lot safer.

Being careful and thoughtful when you buy products that you are going to use in your home and ensuring that they conform to the highest possible standards of safety and manufacture, is tackling the question of home safety at the 'design' stage.

Throughout this book, the term 'home' is used extensively. In referring to your home, we are talking about the immediate area in which you live. This is different to your place of work, which for most of us will be one permanent site or premises. Home also means more than just your domestic building or house. When you are staying with relatives, their home will in effect become your home. Likewise, when you are on holiday, your hotel, caravan or tent becomes your home.

As with any social structure or mechanism, your home is a series of systems. You will have systems for supplying essential services such as water, electricity and gas. You will have systems for supplying yourself with food, and a system for cooking it. You will even have systems for leisure. If you enjoy gardening, then working in your garden will be part of your living system. In a way, you will be as much 'in your home' when you are in the garden as you are when you are in your house. The same is true when you are enjoying a picnic in the countryside, or sitting by the bank of a river fishing.

Simply applying a list of rules and regulations to all these different activities and features of your home life is not necessarily going to make them completely safe. It is much better to catch them at the earliest possible stage, and design the rules into them.

To give a typical example, one hazard that causes many serious accidents in the home is that of glass doors. When the light is poor, or if your mind is perhaps not fully alert, you can walk into glass doors. This is often done by people turning into internal glass panes with their elbow. If the glass shatters, it can cause very grave cuts and injuries.

So how are you to tackle such a hazard in your home? Internal doors are seen by many people as an essential part of their domestic system. As with most other hazards, you can attempt to eliminate them by simply applying a set of rules. Glass is dangerous largely because it is transparent. Therefore you could increase its visibility by sticking things, such as strips of white plastic, to the surface of glass contained in internal doors. Equally you could, perhaps, sub-divide the area of glass into smaller sections with easily-visible horizontal and vertical strips or frames, or you could ensure that the glass is permanently well-lit, and thus more visible.

However, none of these actually make an interior glass door completely safe. No matter how well-lit or visible the glass door is, it would still be possible for somebody to slip and fall against it. Of course, the same could be said of windows, but people do not tend to move towards windows with either the speed or the regularity that they do towards interior doors.

The only way to make such a door completely safe is to design safety into it. In this particular case, that could only mean replacing the door with a solid one, perhaps made of wood. If you felt you desperately needed a glass door, it would have to be both of toughened and opaque glass to fulfil the same requirements. In essence, this is designing safety into your environment. The earlier in the system that you introduce this, the easier it becomes. If you are in a position to decide what types of interior doors you want at the building stage of your house, you save yourself the problem of changing a door at a later stage and thus avoid the expense which that entails. If you do have to change a door, then you will at least remove a hazard and avoid the problem of having to protect permanently a feature of your home with safety precautions and rules.

Of course, the idea of designing safety into your day-to-day living applies to more things than just glass doors. Every time that you identify something as hazardous, you should ask yourself if you could not achieve the same ends with a process that is not as risky.

There is an old rule in industry that if a process is dangerous, then you should try to substitute it with one that is safer. If that is not possible, then you should try to isolate the process as completely as possible. If even that is impossible, then, and only then, you should try to protect yourself from the risks.

In many ways, this is what you should try to do at home. Taking a process that is dangerous and protecting yourself from it would be the very last resort. Instead, every time you decide to do or make something, you should ask yourself in advance what the risks could possibly be and whether you could avoid them by adopting another method. Safety then becomes a philosophy of living rather than a series of checklists that actually complicate things and perhaps even spoil some of your enjoyment when you are passing through your life at home.

It is not possible for one book alone to give you all the precautions associated with every single process that you might use at home and with every way that you might use them. All that we can do here is offer general advice on the different activities that you are likely to pursue at home. If you follow all of them, then you will make your life at home much safer, but complete safety without the unattractive complication of troublesome precautions and questions is something that you must engineer for yourself. We hope that in some way this book will help you to arrive at a balance that allows you to enjoy fully your life at home, and yet to enjoy it as safely as reasonably possible.

And now we come to the eternal quandary facing anybody producing a book on safety. Should a study of how to avoid accidents include advice on what to do if one occurs anyway? In other words, should a book such as this include a section on first aid? Many people would say that a first aid section in a safety book is similar to a football team giving in before the game has started. If you are offering authoritative advice on how to avoid accidents, they might say, then you will not need to tell people what to do if an accident occurs; an accident simply should not be allowed to happen. We take a different view.

Only in a perfect world could accidents be avoided altogether. Even if you are able to completely protect yourself from your own stupidity, you cannot always protect yourself from the stupidity of the people around you! If a risk exists, then the safety-conscious person will attempt to avoid or minimise it. Likewise, if an accident occurs, the safety-conscious person will want to minimise the effect of any injuries. This is caring for the health, safety and welfare of yourself, your family and your neighbours.

Because of this we have included a general section on first

aid (or immediate care, as it is increasingly becoming known) at the end of the book. This is only a rough guide on what to do 'until the ambulance arrives'. We hope that you will supplement this information with knowledge which you can gain from any of the detailed first-aid training courses offered by the first-aid societies or, in all probability, by your local education authority. But most of all, we hope that you will never need to use any knowledge of first aid at all.

# ELECTRICITY

It has often been suggested that early man was introduced to fire by electricity in the form of lightning striking a tree or shrub. Whether or not this is true it is impossible to say, but we certainly knew of electricity for many thousands of years before we learned to harness its potential and before we understood its nature or physics.

But within the last few decades, electricity has become increasingly essential for our day-to-day comfort and entertainment. The list of domestic, industrial and leisure equipment requiring electricity to function is too long to even consider reproducing here, but it is no exaggeration to say that modern men and women rely upon electricity as an energy source more than any other utility or service.

The dangers of electricity in a domestic supply can be broadly separated into two categories: electrocution and fire. Of these, fire is by far the greater hazard. In the HASS (Home Accident Surveillance System) report for 1984, 17 non-fatal cases of electrocution were reported, which only amounted to 0.1 per cent of the total number of domestic injuries. Nationwide, electrocution causes the deaths of about 50 people every year at work. In 1983, 44 people were killed this way in domestic accidents.

Once we look at the figures for fire, however, the conclusions become more startling. As we fill our houses with more and more electrical gadgetry, so we increase the chances of one or another appliance developing a fault and starting a fire. Indeed, in 1950 there were only about 7,000 reported fires where the cause was identified as electrical, but by 1970 the figure had risen to 17,000, and by 1980 to 35,000. Of course, improved techniques for detecting the cause of a fire account for some of this increase, but the basic conclusion remains valid: more and more domestic fires are being started by faulty electrical appliances.

Both the human and the financial costs of fires started by electricity are great. According to government figures, nearly half of all domestic fires are caused by household electrical equipment. During 1983, 173 people died and 2,268 people were injured by fires of this sort, and Home Office figures show that the cost of all fires in the United Kingdom has risen from £20 million in 1950 to a staggering £450 million in 1980. Much of this wastage arises from accidents in industry and commerce, but fires in the home account for a significant proportion of the total.

So electrical safety must be approached with both the hazard of electrocution and the hazard of fire in mind. In some cases the same precautions will protect us from both. Failing to ensure that you put the right fuse in an appliance, for instance, could present both an electrocution and a fire hazard. In other cases however, separate rules will be needed for the two risks. To give just one example, leaving an electric fire in a position where something flammable can fall into it is primarily a fire risk, and would need very much the same rules as any other open fire, whether it should be oil, gas or coal. Areas such as this are examined in the section on Fire Safety, but it again shows how inseparable the different areas of home safety can be.

Before looking at individual areas of electrical safety in the house, it is a good idea to understand a little more about the mains current in Britain and how it is produced and distributed. Electricity is basically produced by a conductor (something that electricity can pass through) rotating inside a magnetic field. This happens on a massive scale inside power stations fuelled, in Britain, by oil, coal, water or atomic energy.

The natural current produced by this process does not, as might be assumed, have a consistent value and charge, but instead pulsates. This is described as an 'alternating current' (ac). As the current-producing conductor turns for one complete revolution inside its magnetic field, the value of the electric current produced will rise to its maximum on one side (positive), then fall back to zero, then rise to its maximum value on the other side (negative). In other words, the term 'live' for the current-supplying wire in an alternating current supply does not mean 'positive', as it will be both positive and negative in rotation as the current pulsates.

In the United Kingdom, domestic supplies are almost exclusively alternating current. You will not be able to detect the alternations in the current, as these occur at a frequency of 50 times every second (50 hertz).

The other current form sometimes used is direct current (dc). This has a constant value above zero, but is actually an alternating current rectified to behave in that way. Because of this fact, direct current is usually only used for certain specialised industrial processes and not for domestic supplies.

After production at power stations, the current is transmitted through overhead lines on pylons at one of three voltages: 400,000 volts, 232,00 volts, or 132,000 volts (400 kV, 232 kV or 132 kV). These massive supplies are taken to substations where they can be transformed down to the voltages required by consumers. In the case of domestic supplies, this is 240 volts (240 V).

The current that you receive travels through carefully organised circuits that allow it to pass from your mains through the live (brown) wire to an appliance, make the appliance function, and then return to the mains through the neutral wire (blue). Electricity will always return to earth if given the chance, so many appliances have a wire connected to their metal parts which, in the event of an electrical fault allowing the current to pass from the live (brown) wire into the casing, will enable the current to pass safely to the earth. This wire (the earth wire) is green and yellow. If you still have old-fashioned wiring on any of your appliances, then the wires may be different colours. The old colours are red for the live wire, black for the neutral wire, and green for the earth.

It is important to remember that some materials are easy for electricity to pass through (conductors), whilst others are hard for it to pass through (insulators). Plastic and rubber are both good insulators, which is why current-carrying wires are coated with plastic. Metals are good conductors, which is why the wires themselves are usually made of a material such as copper. It is also important to remember that, with very high voltages, almost any material can either conduct the current, or be 'jumped' by the current passing through the air.

In the United Kingdom, an extra-high voltage is normally defined as one over 3,000 volts, a high voltage as one between 650 and 3,000 volts, a medium voltage as one between 250 and 650 volts, and a low voltage as one of 250 volts or less. You may sometimes see the old-fashioned word 'pressure' used instead of voltage.

Even with a domestic supply, electricity will be able to pass through the human body, causing the condition described as electrocution. This can easily be fatal (see p.190). For this to happen, your body must complete a circuit. For example, imagine that your electric fire has neither been earthed nor fused correctly, and develops an internal fault in which a live wire touches the inside of the casing. This could well make the outside of the fire live. If you touch it, the current could pass through you and into the earth. You would then be a conductor (although not a good one) and would be completing a circuit for the electricity to flow through. This is known as indirect contact. On a rather more obvious level, you might touch the live wire itself. The effect would be the same, but this would be described as direct contact.

In general, the effects of an alternating current are worse than those of a direct current. This is for a number of reasons. For instance, a pulsating current may cause your muscles to go into spasm with the result that you are not capable of moving the part of your body that is in contact with the source of the current. This is where the erroneous image of people 'sticking' to things that are electrocuting them originates. This phenomenon (sometimes known as the 'involuntary grip') can mean that you receive a longer period of shock than you would do with a direct current.

The level of current which will cause you serious damage is very difficult to determine. An extremely minor current might cause enough of a jolt to startle someone into falling off a ladder and thus indirectly prove fatal. But generally it is a measurement of current in milliamps (mA) that gives an average tolerance threshold for the human body. Presuming a resistance of 1,000 ohms (the measurement used for resistance) and ignoring features such as the extra insulation offered by clothing or footwear, currents above 50 mA can prove fatal.

**To put this into perspective, you would receive a current of 240 mA from a domestic mains supply of 240 volts, and consequently your mains supply is potentially very dangerous indeed.**

The overriding consideration regarding electrical safety in the home is therefore to protect yourself from the current at all times. This is achieved at three centres: the mains, the plug or socket, and the appliance itself. If you are in any doubt how to proceed, consult either a fully qualified electrician or take advice from your area electricity board. Your local fire brigade will advise you on fire safety where electricity is concerned.

Before looking at specific appliances or situations, certain general areas of electrical safety need to be examined. These include: earthing, insulation, fusing, plugs, adaptors and portable sockets.

# Earthing

As explained earlier, the earth connection on an appliance could save your life. In the modern colour coding system, the earth wire is green and yellow. In the old system it was simply green. It is essential that this wire be properly connected at both ends of the flex, and that it be in good condition. You can check this for yourself at the plug end; also check that the plug has been wired safely. If they require earthing (see p.19), most modern appliances made by reputable manufacturers will already be correctly earthed internally. If you have any doubts about the earthing inside an appliance, it is important to ask a qualified electrician to check it for you.

The earth is usually screwed or welded to the inside of the metal casing of the appliance. In the majority of cases the earth inside the appliance will join the earth wire of the flex by a connecting screw similar to that inside the plug and so checking the internal earthing will probably be difficult without removing part or all of the casing. Unless you are quite sure of what you are doing, this is definitely a job for the professional.

## Mains earthing

The circuits that supply current to your power points and to certain specific appliances such as cookers will also be earthed, but since these wires will be hidden by your skirting boards, floorboards or walls, the earth will often be simply a bare copper wire.

In many older houses the mains earth was originally connected to the building's water pipes for the simple, and at that time quite sensible reason that water pipes guaranteed a good, deep and conducting route to the earth. The possibility always exists, however, that sections of those pipes may have been replaced with plastic piping, or even removed altogether. A change such as this might break the earth circuit and thus render the earthing of your appliances ineffective.

If you think this may have occurred, then get a good electrician to check your house wiring.

## Appliances

With some appliances you may find that there is no earth. This is often the case with lights and lighting circuits where the power consumed is very low, and is sometimes the case with other similar, low-power appliances or with appliances that have no metal casings that could become live. In these instances, it is doubly important to ensure the correct fuse rating in the plug and at the main fuse panel. Under no circumstances use a two-core flex for an appliance that should be earthed, or a three-core flex for one that should not be earthed.

One final and important point about earthing must be made. Just as the earth, if it properly and sensibly used, could save your life, it could on the other hand put it at risk if you do not ensure that it is efficiently and safely wired and maintained. If the earth wire in the plug were to work loose and touch the live terminal, it could make any metal parts of the casing live. This can be avoided by ensuring that the plug is correctly and tightly wired up (see p.25).

# Insulation

One of the best ways to prevent electrocution is to make sure that current-carrying wires or apparatus are enclosed in a material that cannot itself conduct current. This is principally why external wires are enclosed in plastic and electrical equipment enclosed in casings. Where the casing is metal, the rules of earthing are very important.

**It is extremely important to maintain both the efficiency and the quality of insulating materials. If the casing of a particular piece of electrical equipment is damaged or ill-fitting, contact the manufacturer or supplier to find the best way to have it repaired. Do not operate the equipment until this has been properly done. Never operate any equipment whilst the casing is removed.**

## Electricians

If you do need to call in an electrician either to replace or to repair a casing, or for any other electrical work, try to select one who is on the roll of the National Inspection Council for Electrical Installation Contracting (NICEIC) or the Electrical Contractors' Association.

## Casings

In certain appliances, casing must be perforated to perform properly. Usually, the reason for this is to allow ventilation. Typical examples of this are radios and television sets. With appliances such as convector heaters, the reason is basically the same, even though the production of heat and its distribution are the main functions of the equipment. With such casings, you must respect two things: that the perforations are a breach in the insulation, and that they must be kept clear for the proper and safe working of the apparatus.

**With this in mind, you must never put anything into or over the vents whilst the equipment is operating. If for any reason it is necessary for you to put anything into or over the**

**vents, ensure that the appliance has been both disconnected from its power supply and allowed sufficient time to cool off completely.**

Never leave equipment of this sort near anything that could fall over or into it. Obvious positions of danger include under fish tanks, near plants that are sometimes watered, under working surfaces or coffee tables, and so on. Needless to say, such equipment should be kept out of the reach of children. If you do spill something into electrical equipment, such as a drink, switch it off and disconnect the plug immediately. Do not switch off at the appliance itself, but at the wall plug. Equally, do not simply wait for the equipment to dry out before switching it on again, but get it professionally serviced.

With equipment such as television sets, where a very high voltage can be used at times, it is extremely important to ensure that there is adequate ventilation and that the perforated areas (usually at the back) are kept clear.

Never hang clothes on, or over, fires or radiators to dry out and never hang them in a position where they could fall onto fires or radiators.

## Flexes

Insulation of current-carrying wires is also important. Always ensure that flexes are in good condition and that they have not frayed. Do not rely upon electrician's insulating tape to mend split or broken flexes and never join wires with *ad hoc* taped junctions. The rubber coating on some older flexes may have perished, especially where the appliance gets hot (as in an electric iron). In general, avoid flexes that are too long for their requirements for these could cause trips or falls. Never try to replace a worn or frayed flex unless you are absolutely sure of what you are doing. If you are going to replace a flex yourself, you can purchase as much cable as you need from most hardware or electrical shops. They will provide you with the flex from a bulk drum or roll, usually at a fixed cost per metre.

Make sure that you tell your supplier both the maximum wattage and the type of appliance that you want the flex for so that he can provide you with a length of the correct rating.

When you disconnect the old flex from the appliance, it is important that you work in an organised and methodical manner. It is a good idea to draw thumbnail sketches of the arrangement of screws, washers and wires before you remove them. This makes the job of reassembling the appliance much simpler. Also sketch the order of the connections so that you can be double sure that you reconnect the new flex correctly. Always label the top of any diagram so that you know that it is the right way up – humorous though it may seem, it is quite easy to get confused with such diagrams, especially if circumstances prevent you from completing the work for a day or two.

Always reserve yourself a clear working space on which to put small things, such as washers and nuts, as you remove them. Try to put them down in the same order that you take them off. This will also make the job of reassembly easier. Remember too that instead of the modern colour coding (Earth: green and yellow, Live: brown, Neutral: blue), an old or worn flex might have the previous coding (Earth: green, Live: red, Neutral: black).

When wiring either a plug or an appliance to a flex, do not remove more of the insulation from each of the wires than is necessary to securely fix the bare part into the terminal.

## Double insulation

If you are purchasing electrical equipment or machines, you may well be able to buy something that is 'double insulated'. This is a technical term for an item of electrical equipment which has internal safety systems offering extra protection for the user.

Equipment such as this is usually portable, such as an electric drill, and will generally only have a two-core lead – the earth is unnecessary. Properly double-insulated appliances will carry a symbol of two or more concentric squares. Follow the manufacturers' instructions very carefully when wiring and fusing such appliances.

# Fusing

In simple terms, a fuse is a length of wire designed to melt at a certain level of current flow. The live wire is broken at the plug, at the mains and sometimes at the appliance itself by a fuse of some sort. This will melt and break the circuit if there is a surge of current. This could be caused by an electrical fault or short-circuit, or the current flowing to earth. Increasingly, automatic circuit breakers are being used instead of fuses. Whilst these are not strictly fuses, their purpose and effect are the same, so they will also be examined here.

Fuses must be balanced for a specific appliance. An electric fire will need a 13 A fuse in its plug because it requires a considerable current to operate and often a much larger one to start from cold. An electric light, however, needs much less power, and consequently should have a lower value fuse.

## Fuse rating

**Ensuring that fuses are properly rated is essential. If you 'overfuse' something, which means giving it a fuse rated higher than the current it consumes, the fuse might allow the current to flow to earth without melting as it should. This would endanger anybody who touched a live part and would damage the machine itself in the case of a fault. It would also present a considerable fire hazard. Choosing the correct fuse is an essential step where ensuring electrical safety is concerned.**

Fuses or circuit breakers will be fitted at two points in your electrical system: the main fuse panel and the plugs.

When fitting fuses into plugs you must follow the manufacturers' recommendations exactly. Plugs that you buy will probably already carry a 13 A cartridge fuse. This is simply a length of fuse wire held between two metal terminals and enclosed in a ceramic cylinder. Depending upon the nature of the appliance, you may have to change this fuse to one with a lower rating. These can be bought cheaply from most hardware or electrical goods shops.

## Cartridge fuses

Cartridge fuses come in a variety of ratings, usually from 1 A to 30 A, although you will probably only encounter 3, 5 and 13 A fuses, which cover most household appliances. Smaller ratings are used for such things as clock connections and shaver sockets, and ratings higher than 13 A are usually used for things such as cooker units.

Fuses that you buy to use with alternating currents should conform to BS 1361 or to BS 1362.

It is not possible to provide a comprehensive guide to the fuse ratings which should be used for each type of appliance. For instance, a television set might run at a power rating of 700 watts which should be adequately catered for by a 3 A fuse; however it could (and in many cases would) require a far greater surge of power to actually get started when you turn it on. Many household electrical appliances share this surge phenomenon; unless you are qualified to calculate the safe fusing for an item, you must consult an electrician or your electricity board. With new items, follow the manufacturers' advice.

**Remember the prime rule of electrical fusing: it is always dangerous to play guessing games with electricity, but in the case of fuses, it is far, far more dangerous to overfuse than it is to underfuse. Even some manufacturers of fuses in Britain refuse to offer general guidelines for matching fuses to appliances, so it is unlikely that you will always be able to guess the correct rating yourself. If you are in any doubt, use a lower rather than higher rated fuse, but ideally consult a professional.**

## Circuit breakers

At the mains panel, miniature circuit breakers (MCBs) are increasingly being used in place of the traditional rewireable or cartridge fuses. With these, a current surge will switch off the circuit. When the fault has been identified, the circuit can simply be switched back on again. This saves time, and is more convenient than stumbling around in your cellar with a torch. Miniature circuit breakers work well for domestic mains circuits, but will probably need backing up with another method of fusing. They should conform to BS 3871.

## Mains panels

If you do blow a fuse at your mains panel, disconnect the mains supply by turning off its switch, which should be situated on the panel itself. If your fuses are of the rewireable type, remove and examine each one in turn until you discover the fuse that has blown. This will have melted through, and may have scorch marks on its carrier. Loosen the connection screws on the carrier and remove the ends of the old fuse wire.

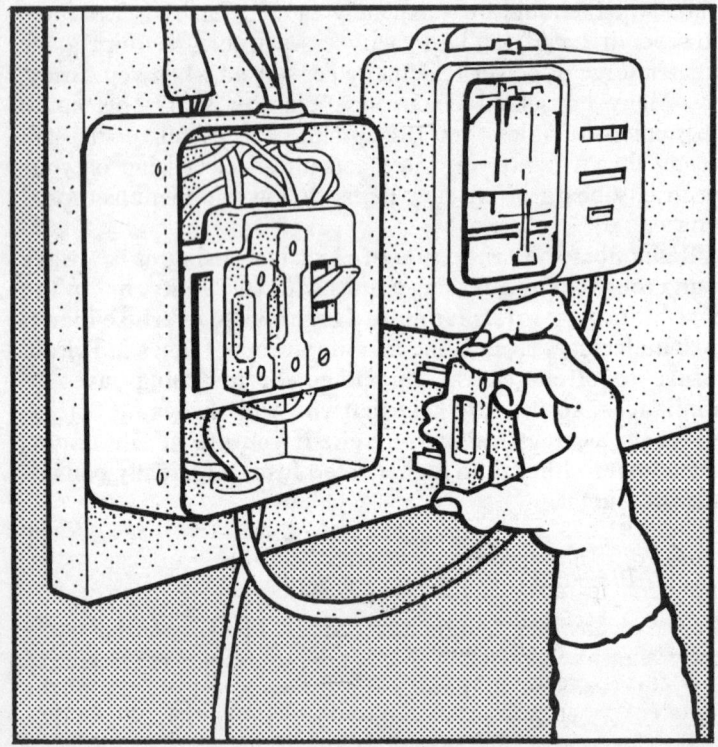

Correctly rated mains fuses are essential

Replace the wire with a short length of new fuse wire of the correct rating. The rating should be printed on the back of the carrier, and will be in amps. Only use proper fuse wire, which can be bought from most hardware or electrical shops, and use enough for the wire to be slightly slack once it is in place. Put the carrier back into the panel and replace any cases or covers that you have taken off before switching the mains back on again. You may find that the carrier has a distinctive marking such as a coloured dot on its back to indicate which way up it should go. This should be matched with those on the other carriers.

If your mains panel contains cartridge fuses, as many do, switch off the mains supply and remove the offending carrier. Unscrew its two parts and remove the cartridge fuse from inside. Check that the fuse is intact. If it is not, replace it with a fuse of the same rating. It is worth noting that lighting circuits are usually covered by 5 A fuses (white), and the power points by 30 A fuses (red). You can buy special screwdrivers that enable you to check whether a fuse is functioning or not.

Many things can cause mains fuses to blow, including a surge in the current, a short circuit or fault in an appliance, or a defect in the fuse itself. Sometimes a fuse will blow for no apparent reason and will be fine once replaced, but if your fuses keep blowing after you replace them, seek professional advice.

## Earth leakage circuit breakers

One of the more modern innovations for domestic (and, for that matter, industrial) fusing is the Earth Leakage Circuit Breaker (ELCB). Earlier versions of this were voltage operated and did not prove completely reliable but the newer, current-operated ELCBs are extremely sensitive and safe. If you are having these fitted, you may need two, one for your lighting and one for your power circuits. As these are sensitive to current leaking to earth, which is the usual passage of current when somebody is being electrocuted, they offer a good level of general personal protection.

If your ELCB 'trips' and disconnects the supply, reset the

trip. If it continues to trip, you can easily discover the exact cause of the fault. Firstly, switch off and disconnect all appliances covered by the ELCB and again reset the trip. One by one plug in the appliances and switch them on. As soon as you switch on the faulty appliance, the ELCB will trip again.

It is now possible to buy plugs or adaptors fitted with ELCBs, or Residual Current Circuit Breakers (RCCBs) as they are increasingly becoming known. These can be used to protect specific appliances without the expense of having them fitted to cover your entire house mains.

# Plugs

Apart from units such as electric cookers, immersion heaters and storage heaters, which are often wired straight into your house circuits, most appliances you use will need to have an electric plug fitted to the end of their flex. As explained earlier, all plugs should conform to BS 1363, and normally should be 'square-pin'. This means that the three pins that connect into the power point should be rectangular in cross-section. The old-fashioned round-pin plugs are rarely used now. Having said that, they are still sometimes used for domestic supplies, especially in halls of residence and other similar buildings. If you do have to buy round-pin plugs for your appliances the rules for wiring them are basically the same as those for square-pin plugs, but you must be particularly careful when choosing them.

New round-pin plugs are not always easy to buy in this country, with the result that some of those on sale have been manufactured in the Far East. Try to avoid these if you can. If necessary, contact one of the plug manufacturers or one of the safety organisations at the end of this book for advice.

In general, a square-pin plug will be the type that you use. Note that the top pin, which is the earth, is longer than the other two, which are the live and neutral pins. This is because the live and neutral holes in your socket are covered by a protective shield to prevent children sticking anything in. This shield is lifted by the earth pin as the plug is pushed in.

It has been said repeatedly that you should seek professional advice whenever you are in doubt about any electrical matters, but changing a plug or its fuse should not be beyond your capabilities. By observing the following rules, you can do it safely and securely, and save yourself unnecessary expenditure.

Always remember – one appliance, one plug. Never try to fix flexes into a power point using matches or by poking the bare wires into the holes. This is one of the surest ways to kill yourself. Equally, never try to connect two or more flexes to the same plug. If you have to use two appliances in the same socket, use a high-quality adaptor or a multiple socket (see p.29), but always follow the 'one appliance, one plug' rule.

## Fitting a plug

Proceed in a methodical manner with your tools gathered in advance. You will need an electrican's screwdriver, a slightly larger screwdriver to remove the casing and to loosen the grip screws, and a sharp knife to remove the insulation from the wires. It is a good idea to buy a pair of wire strippers. These are fairly inexpensive and can be bought from most electrical shops.

Buy a 13 A plug conforming to BS 1363. Determine the correct fuse rating for the appliance you are going to fit the plug to. If this is not clear on the appliance itself, then ask your dealer when you buy the plug. If the rating is lower than 13 A, then buy a new fuse as well.

Remove two inches from the end of the outer casing of the flex leaving the three plastic-coated wires inside exposed. If you do this with a knife be careful not to cut or damage the insulation around the inner wires. Remove the back casing from the plug. There will be either one or two screws in the face of the plug that you must remove or loosen to do this. If you have to remove them, place them safely aside.

As you look at the back of the plug, which will now be exposed, the earth terminal will be by itself at the top (marked E), the live will be at the bottom right at one end of the fuse (marked L), and the neutral will be at the bottom left (marked N). These will probably also have their colour codings written by them. Remember again that if your flex is old, it may still have the old colour coding.

At the very bottom of the plug there will be either a small fibrous strip held down by two screws, which should be removed, or a slot between two pieces of plastic. This is the cord or cable grip and should, if possible, grip the outer casing of your flex. Place the last few millimetres of outer casing against the cord grip and trim the inner wires individually to the right length to reach the back of their respective terminals. When calculating this length, remember that you do not want the wires so long that you have to curl or buckle them to fit them in, nor so short that they cannot easily follow the path of the moulded conduit provided for them. Also allow for the fact

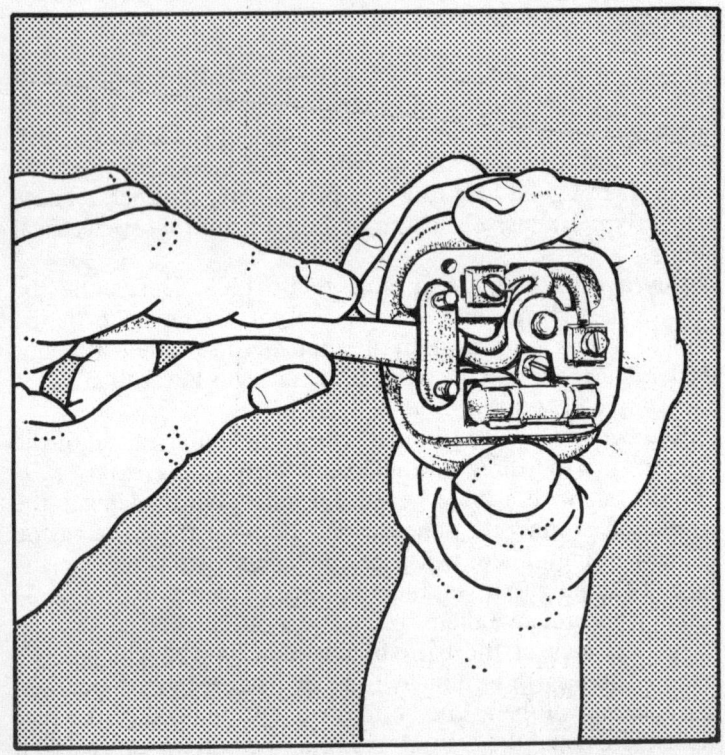

When wiring a plug, check that the cord grip is holding firmly

that a quarter of an inch of the end of each wire will be stripped to go into each terminal. You will find that the earth wire needs to be longer than the other two.

Strip the last quarter of an inch or so of each wire to expose the metal strands inside. Biting such things as wire, thread or fishing line can cause abscessed teeth, so do this with a pair of pliers or wire strippers. Now twist the strands of each wire in turn between your fingers to plait them into a single core. One by one loosen the screws in the terminals, push the bare part of the appropriate wire completely into the hole and tighten the screw down firmly. If necessary you can pull the pin out of its hole to do this, but tighten the screw down again after you have put the pin back. You may also find it easier to remove the fuse before connecting the live wire.

After this, fit the flex into the cable grip. If the latter is a slot, push the flex well down into it. If it is a fibrous strip, tighten the wires down firmly to trap the cable.

Before you replace the plug casing, check:
1. **That all terminals have been tightly screwed down.**
2. **That no bare wire is showing, and no individual strands are sticking out.**
3. **That the fuse is the correct rating for the appliance.**
4. **That the flex is securely held in the cable grip. Pinch the flex between two fingers and tug it sideways to check this.**

Now you can screw back the outer casing of the plug and use the appliance.

With table lamps and some other low-power or double-insulated equipment there may be no earth wire in the flex. The inner wires will probably still be coloured blue and brown, and should be connected as normal. Check that the screw on the empty earth terminal is also tightly screwed down before reassembling the plug. With some lighting flexes, the two wires are the same colour and are not in an outer casing, but instead are fused together by their individual plastic coatings. With these, connect one wire to the neutral and one to the live terminals; it does not matter which goes to which. These cables are only to be used for low-power appliances with a low fuse rating, and should not, for instance, be used with a double-insulated hair drier or any other higher powered two-core appliance.

## Changing a fuse

The procedure is the same as for changing a plug, except that you do not need to touch the flex or terminals at all. However, it does allow an opportunity to check that the wiring is in good condition and that everything is screwed down firmly. You should also, of course, make sure that the fuse you put in is of the correct rating. Do not rely upon the old fuse to tell you; the person who originally wired the plug may not have been as careful as they should.

# Power points, adaptors, sockets and switches

Your home will probably not have a sufficient number of power points for your needs, especially if it is an older building. Some reports suggest that people in general require a total of 34 sockets, with at least ten of these in the kitchen. There are various ways of connecting more than one appliance to each socket, but these are at best a temporary solution and at worst are potentially dangerous.

**Each power point in your home designed to supply power to a square-pin plug should be capable of handling a current of 13 amperes (13 A) at 240 volts (240 V). The power that this represents is calculated by multiplying the number of amps by the number of volts. This shows that the socket is capable of handling a maximum of just over 3,000 watts (3 kW) in total. If you expect the socket to supply more than that amount, then you will be overloading the power point and may run the risk of developing an electrical fault or starting a fire.**

## Power ratings

It is therefore important to be sure of the power ratings of different appliances in your house. This will normally be printed on them, but a good general guide is: televisions, fridges, coffee makers, vacuum cleaners, microwave ovens, hair driers, freezers, food mixers, most DIY equipment, video and stereo equipment, lamps and home computers – 1,200 watts or less. Washing machines, tumble driers, electric irons and toasters – between 1,200 watts and 2,500 watts. Radiant heaters (or bar fires), fan heaters and electric kettles – up to a maximum of 3,000 watts. If you are in any doubt about the wattage of a particular appliance consult the manufacturer, supplier or an electrician. For the reasons given earlier (see p.21) this guide does not necessarily indicate the fuse rating of different appliances accurately.

## Adaptors and sockets

You can use portable adaptors or portable sockets to enable you to connect more than one appliance to each socket, but count up the wattages to check that they total 3,000 watts or less. For instance, a table lamp, hi-fi, video recorder and fridge could all in theory operate off the same socket simultaneously and yet consume under 500 watts, whilst a three-bar electric fire functioning with a toaster would dangerously overload the circuit. You must check these yourself.

If you buy adaptors or portable sockets, make sure that they conform to BS 1363 and that, if possible, they are made in Britain. Also, try to select those that are fused internally.

Never plug one adaptor into another to convert one wall socket into three. Quite apart from the risks of overloading, or of people tripping over the tangle of wires, the weight of the unit could pull itself sufficiently out of the socket for a child to squeeze its fingers behind and touch one of the pins. You may well find that a better long-term solution is to have a multi-socket fitted to your wall. Whilst portable sockets usually only have a maximum of four outlets (described as 4-gang), multi-sockets can have anything up to six outlets. These can either be wired into your existing circuit or given a new one of their own. They can be wired so that each individual outlet is capable of supplying up to 3,000 watts and this is a very good way to avoid overloading. Unless you are skilled and confident, ask an electrician to do this for you.

If you want to do the job as safely and thoroughly as possible, you may feel it wise to add normal one- or two-outlet sockets to your domestic circuits throughout the house.

A multi-socket will solve the problem of too few sockets in one immediate working area, but is not the best solution for every situation. You may feel that you need six outlets in every room of your house, which would be quite reasonable, but it is unlikely that you would want to run six appliances in the same part of every room. This is why power points are placed at intervals around the skirting or walls of your rooms, and not clustered together. One possible result of using multi-sockets in every situation is that you would end up with flexes trailing across floors or rooms. This is undesirable for the obvious reason that people can trip or fall over them. So one way both to fulfil your power requirements and to design safety into your environment is to consider fitting more sockets.

## Fitting sockets and switches

Legally, there is nothing to prevent you from rewiring your own home, although you must have your work checked after you have finished, but it is a difficult and demanding thing to do.

**If you decide to rewire all or part of your home, consult your electricity board for advice and work carefully from an authoritative book or instruction manual. Even with comparatively minor work such as adding sockets to existing circuits, get a professional to check that it is safe when the work is completed.**

But whether you are employing someone to do the work for you, or are doing it yourself, it is you who must design the changes that you would like to see. Prevailing standards only require a minimum of 17 power points in new houses, and it is likely that you will need more than that. If you have just moved into a new house, do not rush into adding extra sockets, instead wait until experience shows you where additional power points would be desirable. Walk from one room to the next writing down the number of extra sockets you would like, and where you would like them. Also decide now whether you would prefer double or single sockets in each instance. Tend if anything to over-estimate your requirements. This will allow you the freedom to alter the arrangement of furniture in your rooms and yet still have plenty of accessible power points.

Your house will almost certainly be wired with 'ring' circuits. In these, the cable runs from the mains in a ring passing through every power point and then back. You will probably have a separate ring circuit for every floor of your house and may have one for the kitchen as well. Your electrician will either put the extra sockets straight into the ring, or run a branch or 'spur' line off the main ring.

You can have as many fused spurs running off your main ring as you wish, but do bear in mind that most main rings are covered by a 30 A fuse. The same equation as used earlier (current × voltage) therefore gives a power capacity of 7,200 watts and means that the circuit can support appliances of a total power rating of 7,200 watts, all running at once. Whilst this sounds a lot, too many power points in use simultaneously could overload the circuit, so it might be sensible to have a new ring put in if you feel that this could be a possibility in your case. Your electrician will advise you on this question. It is worth noting that the Wiring Regulations prohibit you from using more unfused spurs than you have existing sockets in the main ring.

**If your wiring is old, it might be wise to have it completely redone. Danger signs include mains cables in insulating covers of rubber or anything else other than PVC; Bakelite (old-fashioned brown plastic) sockets, plugs or fittings; round-pin plugs and sockets rated for different currents (i.e. 15 A, 5 A or 2 A), or metal conduiting (the tubes or troughs used to run cables through on, for instance, your walls).**

A rather less satisfactory but cheaper way to increase the number of sockets is to replace single sockets with double outlets. In the majority of cases this will give you an extra outlet with a 3 kW capacity, but occasionally, when the single socket itself is on a spur from a connection unit fused at 13 A, you will only have a total capacity of 3 kW, or 1.5 kW per outlet. Check this with your electrician.

## Sockets and switches

If you are replacing wall sockets, light sockets or light switches, the rules are similar to those for plugs, except that you must always switch off your power at the mains before starting work. With a wall socket, plug a table lamp into the socket before starting. Check that it works. After you have switched off the mains, check that the lamp no longer works in that socket.

**All other wall sockets and lights in the house should also have stopped working when you switched the mains off. If you have any doubts whatsoever and are not entirely confident in your knowledge of electricity, call in a good electrician to do the job for you.**

To remove the old socket, take off the front casing by loosening the fixing screws. The back plate will be fixed to the wall or skirting board by two other, larger screws, which will now be visible. Once the plate is removed, you will see the mains wires coming from the conduit, container box or through a hole in the wall or skirting, depending upon the system used in your house. There will probably be two mains wires, one to go into the socket, and one to go out. This is because your wiring will almost certainly be composed of 'ring' circuits (see p.31). Special appliances such as cookers often have what is described as a 'radial' circuit, but most power points will be on a ring circuit. The wires will follow the same colours as those outlined above for plugs except that the earth may just be a bare copper wire. As an extra precaution, avoid touching any metal wires whilst you are working, and use a good electrician's screwdriver with a rubber-insulated handle.

If you are changing light switches, sockets, or ceiling or wall junctions, you must also switch off the power at the mains. Never take a risk and just turn off the wall switch – somebody or something might accidentally switch it back on again. Whilst lighting flexes are two-core, and may well not have a colour coding (as explained earlier), the mains supply to a light switch or socket should have both a colour coded wire and some form of earthing, either through a metal conduit to which the switch is fixed, or through a proper earth wire. Again, if you are uncertain, seek professional advice.

Because your power and lighting circuits are designed to carry different currents, it is essential never to confuse them. For instance, never attempt to plug anything other than a light bulb into a light socket. Doing things such as powering your television set from a light socket can be extremely dangerous.

Some specific areas of domestic electrical usage and some specific appliances require particular attention.

# The bathroom or shower

Most people know that water conducts electricity. Whilst it is not a good conductor in the way that metals are, it is still important to minimise its contact with electrical appliances, and to ensure that any contact is controlled. We discussed earlier how dangerous it is to put electrical appliances in a position where water or other liquids can fall into them, such as a bar fire under a fish tank, or a vase of flowers standing on a television set. Nowhere are these rules more important than in the bathroom.

The fundamental rules of electrical safety in the bathroom are designed to minimise any possibility of water coming into contact with the current or acting as a conducting bridge between the current and yourself. By and large, the precautions that you should take are self-evident if you remember the manner in which electricity behaves.

## Lighting

Light switches inside the bathroom should be operated with a pull cord, as should wall-mounted electric heaters or lights over mirrors. If you do use a conventional switch for your main light, mount it on the wall outside the bathroom. The Institute of Electrical Engineers (IEE) Wiring Regulations make some specific references to bathrooms and showers. Lights that are within 2.5 m of the bath or shower must be either made of, or insulated by, a material that does not conduct electricity. Bayonet-type lampholders must be fitted with a protective shield. This should conform to BS 5042. As an alternative, you could use totally enclosed luminaires (the technical term for conventional lamps) instead.

## Showers

Electric showers in a bathroom must only be powered by a special shower unit conforming to BS 3052. You must never have normal 13 A sockets in your bathroom. If you have a shower fitted outside your bathroom (in the corner of your bedroom, for instance), then any power points must be at least 2.5 m from the unit.

## Appliances

There are only certain things that you can install so that they are normally within the reach of anybody using the bath or shower. These include electric shaver units, pull cords for switches, and the controls of any instant water heaters that the shower uses. Such heaters must themselves comply with BS 3456. You are also prohibited from installing a wall fire with heating elements within reach of anybody using the bath or shower.

Since the last edition of the regulations (1981), they have been amended to permit the use of various modern types of bathroom equipment such as booster pumps for showers and whirlpool baths. These allow you to have electrical equipment in your bathroom, but only if it functions off a special circuit: the Safety Extra-Low Voltage (SELV) circuit. This confines you to a 12 V ac or dc supply and it must be specially fitted. Normally, you must never take any portable electric equipment such as mains-supplied radios or hair driers into your bathroom, even if they are plugged in outside. With this amendment, however, 12 V appliances would be permitted, provided that they are powered off a 12 V SELV socket.

This is safe because mains-supplied radios or similar low-voltage equipment whilst only using relatively low voltages to function, are normally fed with the mains current which is then transformed internally down to the correct low power. This means that the flex, its sockets into the radio and the transformer part of the radio are all capable of giving a powerful electric shock.

With appliances designed to use a 12 V SELV socket, however, it is a safe, low voltage that actually comes out of the power point, so that you would not be able to give yourself a serious or dangerous shock. For more information about this, consult your electricity board.

However, just because the regulations say that this is a good, safe design to model your bathroom on does not mean that your bathroom actually conforms to it. Check for yourself. If anything does not come up to this high standard – change it. For instance, occasions where people have fixed conventional, portable bar fires to their bathroom walls are not unknown. Nor, for that matter, are the injuries and damage that result from them.

If you design your bathroom to conform to these standards it should be very safe. Only if you carry risks in with you will you threaten that safety. At the risk of becoming repetitive, one of the most dangerous things that people do is to plug a fire, radio, lamp or whatever into a socket outside the bathroom, and then carry the appliance inside, sometimes even standing it on the edge of the bath itself. Do not take that kind of risk.

# The darkroom

It sounds slightly confusing to refer to the darkroom in the same vein as the bathroom. Most of us, of course, do not have photographic darkrooms set up in our homes. But many keen photographers do have one set up and for the very best of reasons. It enables them, amongst other things, to develop and process films more cheaply, more quickly and with more care than through a chemist.

The safety aspects of darkrooms could be examined in the same section as DIY safety, except that few other areas of DIY involve setting up a permanent work space within the house. Even the workshop is usually based in an outbuilding or garage, whereas home darkrooms are almost exclusively inside the house.

Safety precautions in the darkroom are similar to those for the bathroom. Indeed, many people convert their bathrooms into *ad hoc* darkrooms. As with the bathroom, you must avoid any contact between electricity and water. You must, therefore, always dry your hands before switching on any equipment, so keep a supply of fabric or paper towels handy.

One big advantage of designing safety into the darkroom is that its processes can be roughly divided into 'dry and electrical', and 'wet and non-electrical'. These should always be separated by the full length of the room, with a good supply of towels in between. The only exceptions to this are automatic drying machines, whether they are for paper or negatives. If these are made by a reputable manufacturer and properly serviced, fused and wired, they will have their own in-built safety mechanisms designed to deal with the problem of water. Yet again, if in any doubt, contact an electrician. In this case, ask your photographic dealer if he can recommend one.

**It is a good idea to set up a dry bench in the darkroom. Water must never come into contact with this bench, so hang a dry towel near it. Wet processes (including the developer, stop and fix baths) should be on a surface by the sink. Chemicals must also be mixed on that 'wet' bench area.**

The dry bench should carry the enlarger and safe lights. As in the bathroom, main lights should be controlled by a pull cord. The rules of insulating, earthing and fusing apply as fully for the equipment in the darkroom as they do for any other domestic electric appliances.

If you are using the bathroom as a darkroom, you must take certain other precautions. First of all, chemical safety must be considered, and all the rules for handling and disposing of photographic materials have to be followed (see p.164). Secondly, you are not allowed to have 13 A power points in a bath or shower room, so your enlarger, safe lights and extractor fan must be powered from portable sockets plugged in outside the room. These can then be removed once you have finished your photographic work and before anybody else uses the bathroom. This fact alone makes the bathroom a far-from-ideal place to construct your darkroom – the possibility that you might forget to unplug and disconnect your equipment before having a bath is always there. However, the fact is that many people do construct a darkroom in their bathroom, so the responsibility to ensure that this rule is strictly followed lies with them.

Also bear in mind the fact that a hot, steamy atmosphere will not have a beneficial effect on your photographic equipment. It might, therefore, be a good idea to remove the apparatus as well as the portable socket when people wish to use the bath.

# The kitchen

After the bathroom, the kitchen is the room that contains the most hazards. People are using more and more portable electric appliances to do the tasks that were previously done by hand: coffee makers, blenders, slow cookers, microwave ovens, toasters; these and others are now common to many households.

In general, the same basic rules should be followed for these appliances as were outlined earlier: ensure correct fusing, insulation, earthing, usage and servicing. However, one or two specific points should be made.

## *Circuits*

As noted earlier, kitchens will often have their own 'ring main' circuit and a 'radial' circuit for appliances such as electric cookers. This can sometimes mean that your kitchen has an older wiring system than the rest of your house. You must check whether or not this is the case and also whether you have any of the old-fashioned 'bayonet' type adaptors. These are dangerous, as appliances such as electric irons must be properly earthed. If you do have any of these, do not use them. Replace them as soon as possible.

## *Flexes*

Many modern appliances have completely removable flexes. These usually have a plug at one end, and a moulded connector or 'coupler' at the other end. The coupler should conform to BS 4491 and the inlet on the appliance to BS 3283. If possible, purchase appliances where the flex is marked with a Safety Mark.

This type of flex is commonly used for electric kettles. It is extremely important to switch off the appliance and unplug it at the mains before removing the coupler from the inlet. If you do not do this and simply unplug the coupler from the kettle once it has boiled without switching off the power point, the

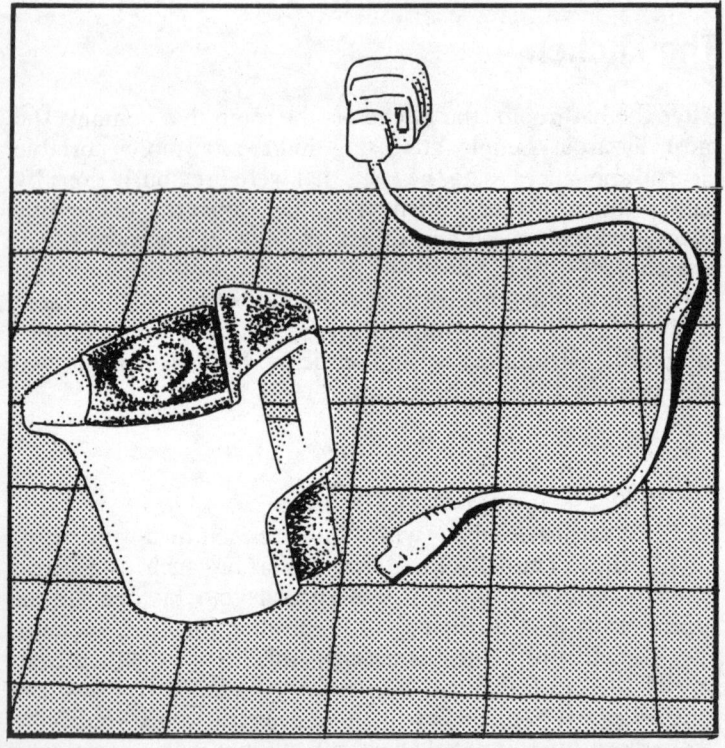

Never leave flexes plugged in at the wall but not at the appliance

coupler end of the flex will still be live and will be capable of giving an electric shock were it to be, for instance, immersed in water. Children will sometimes put things like this into their mouths. Indeed, we know personally of a case where somebody quite incorrectly plugged their electric shaver into a light socket and left it dangling once they had finished with it. Shortly afterwards, their young son put the shaver into his mouth and fatally electrocuted himself. Whilst the analogy is admittedly not exact, it does illustrate the importance of taking all possible precautions.

So electric kettles must always be switched off and unplugged before either filling or pouring; do not rely upon the switch on the appliance alone.

The rules already outlined regarding electrical safety apply just as fully in the kitchen. If an appliance such as an electric toaster becomes blocked, you must unplug it before clearing the blockage. Some kitchen equipment such as cookers, washing machines, dishwashers and fridges have large areas of metal casing, so it is doubly important that you check the earthing and fusing in the plug.

If you use an appliance such as an electric iron, remember that heat can damage the insulation on the flex. Allow the iron to cool down before coiling the flex around it and putting it away. Ideally, you should avoid coiling the flex altogether, and store the iron with the flex loose. When using equipment such as microwave ovens, follow the manufacturer's instructions carefully.

# Television sets

The greatest hazard you are likely to encounter in your living room is your television set. Televisions use a very high voltage, with black and white (or monochromatic) sets generating 10,000 or more volts and colour generating 20,000 or more volts.

Obviously, your mains current does not supply voltages of that magnitude in that form, but your television contains its own circuits designed to convert the supply into the form necessary to power the cathode ray tube (or 'tube') inside it. These voltages can be retained for some time after the set has been switched off.

## Fire

It is important to switch off and unplug your television when it is not in use. Fire is one of the main hazards at this level of voltage. The expression 'warming up' is no misconception where televisions are concerned – many of the internal parts become quite hot whilst the set is functioning, so it is important to ensure that the ventilation holes are kept clear at all times.

**If your television catches fire, or even if you smell burning or see smoke coming from the back, switch it off at the mains. Do not use water or a liquid-based fire extinguisher to put out any flames (see p.63). If you believe the set could be on fire – call your fire brigade.**

Unless you are qualified to do so, never take the back off your television, nor attempt to repair it yourself. The tube in your set contains a vacuum and will therefore 'implode' if it breaks (the opposite of an explosion: the glass will blow inwards). Even so, this can still throw broken glass and cause injuries so if your picture shows any signs of distortion, or develops 'spitting' horizontal lines, switch it off and consult a qualified television repairer.

Never stand fish tanks, vases filled with water, drinks or anything else containing liquid on or above a television set in case it tips into the back and causes a short circuit.

Above all, remember to both switch off and unplug your set every time you stop watching it. During 1983, 12 people were killed in domestic accidents involving televisions, ten of whom died as the result of a fire. This emphasises the importance of unplugging the set when you leave it – do not rely on the switch on the television itself.

# Electric blankets

Most appliances used in the bedroom are adequately covered by the general precautions outlined throughout the earlier part of this section. Indeed, there is only one real exception: that of electric blankets.

Electrically heated blankets have been the subject of such widespread safety campaigns that they are no longer quite the menace that they seemed to have been some years ago. Nonetheless, 14 of the 5,000 fatalities recorded in the 1983 HASS report involved electric blankets, so they should be chosen and used carefully in accordance with the manufacturer's instructions.

When you buy an electric blanket, try to buy one that conforms to BS 3456 (section A4). Avoid buying second-hand blankets. The manufacturers or suppliers may make recommendations regarding the servicing of your blanket – ensure that these are fully complied with. Electric blankets can be divided into two types: underblankets and overblankets. You must always put these to their proper use – never put an underblanket on top or an overblanket underneath.

Some blankets are designed to be used all night. They have a safe, low voltage and will probably cost you a little more than the other types. Check carefully whether your blanket should be switched off and unplugged before you get into bed, or whether it is safe to use it all night. Never attempt to use a wet electric blanket, nor attempt to dry a wet blanket out by switching it on. Never use a hot water bottle with an electric blanket. Underblankets must be fixed securely to the bed, and should be kept flat. Electric blankets should not be folded, as creases or folds can cause overheating.

# Hobbies and toys

Aquaria, electric model railways, home-brew heaters and similar forms of hobby equipment figure in a large proportion of domestic leisure pursuits.

*Safety First*

By and large the general precautions discussed earlier summarise the rules for using electrical hobby equipment and toys. Most of these appliances have a low power rating and will be adequately covered by a 3 A fuse. Indeed, many appliances, such as model railways and electronic calculators, only require between 9 V and 12 V to operate correctly. Apparatus such as this utilises a transformer system to reduce the mains current to that required. Sometimes this takes the form of a mains adaptor and at other times it takes the form of a transformer inside the appliance itself. But in all cases the plug, flex and transformer will carry a mains current, so all due care must be taken.

Aquaria merit a special mention. Few areas of home leisure activity involve a combination of water and electricity to the extent that fish keeping does. An average tropical fish tank will need electric lights, pump, heater and thermostat. These appliances will probably only have two-core flexes, not because they are double-insulated but because their power requirements are very low. Do not abuse this by overfusing them; 3 A fuses will cover all items of aquaria equipment quite adequately. Always switch off and unplug all your apparatus before putting your hands into the water. And for that matter, always dry your hands before switching it back on again. Avoid *ad hoc* assemblages of wires. Buy a proper connector box. These hang on the back of the tank and are usually fused internally.

Some heaters for both aquaria and home-brew use contain a combined heater and thermostat, with the thermostat at the upper end of the glass tube. Be careful that the thermosat is below the water level. If you allow the water level to drop below the level of the thermostat at a time when the air temperature is very cold, then the thermostat may measure the warmth of the air rather than the water and thus fail to cut-out the heater when the water has reached the desired temperature. Quite apart from the danger of this overheating causing an electrical fault, you may well end up with a tank of boiled and extremely dead fish!

# FIRE SAFETY

Losing relatives or property in a fire is one of the most unhappy and unsettling experiences that can confront one in life. Yet despite the apparently high public awareness of the dangers of fire, 60 per cent of all fires in occupied buildings occur in the home, many of which could be avoided if simple precautions and safety checks were followed.

Major disasters involving fire appear particularly shocking, but can sometimes seem remote as well. Everyone who saw the Bradford City Football Club fire in 1985 on their television set will have been shocked by the speed with which the fire consumed the stand and by the intensity of the heat. Other disasters such as the Manchester Woolworths fire, the Star Dust Disco fire in Ireland and the fire at the Summerland leisure complex on the Isle of Man, were equally frightening, but still somehow removed from the environment of your own home and the hazards that it can present. Even some firemen were surprised by the speed of the Bradford fire, but it should be remembered that the normal household can contain the ingredients of just such a fire, albeit on a smaller scale.

**Some modern furnishings contain materials that burn with a temperature of over 1,000 degrees centigrade and give off clouds of deadly poisonous fumes. Under the right circumstances, fires that start in one room can sweep through an entire home within two minutes.**

Fire has always been a major cause of death, injury and property damage in the United Kingdom. Taking 1984 as the most recent year for which Home Office figures are available, we can reveal a frightening picture.

During that year, there were a total of 447,000 fires, of which 101,500 were in occupied buildings, although not all of these were homes. However, 59,000 (60 per cent) of these were in dwellings, that is, in houses, bungalows, flats and such like. Throughout that year alone, 887 people died from fire, of whom the majority (692) died from fires in dwellings. A further 75 died from fires in other occupied buildings and 62 in road vehicle accident fires. In addition to these, there were 11,120 non-fatal casualties, of whom 7,760 were injured in domestic fires and 2,160 in other occupied buildings.

The same statistics can help us to identify the areas of your home where fires are most likely to start. For instance, in 1984 cooking appliances started over 21,000 fires, which is hardly surprising. Other culprits included smokers, space heating appliances (such as gas fires), electric wiring, and electrical equipment in general.

Inevitably, those most at risk from fire in the home are those least able to look after themselves; the very young and the elderly. In 1984 fire caused the deaths of 128 children under 15 years old and of 350 people over 65. A further 3,000 people in these age groups suffered non-fatal injuries. Over twice as many people are killed every year by smoke or fumes as are killed by the flames themselves.

All of this paints a very depressing picture of fire safety in the home. But the figures do have a positive side. In 1984, 29,300 fires were extinguished before the fire brigade arrived, and it was only in 9 per cent of those which occurred in occupied buildings that the fire spread beyond the room in which it started.

Measures can be taken to prevent the spread of fire should it start, to limit its ability to hurt or poison people, and most importantly to prevent it from starting in the first place. But first of all it is necessary to understand the nature of fire: how it starts, how it spreads, and what its effects can be.

# What is fire?

There are few common dangers which inspire as much panic as fire. People tend to assess its threat, quite understandably, in the light of its symptoms; intense heat, toxic fumes, smoke, and its ability to spread. By the time that a fire in your home has actually started, these are indeed the properties of fire that will be most important and relevant to you, and they are examined in detail later. But the field of fire safety is far, far greater than that and, like many other areas of safety, is most relevant before an accident occurs, not afterwards.

Understanding what fire is, and how the physical conditions that are favourable to its starting can be avoided, will enable you to make your home almost free of risk. Of course, external circumstances beyond your control may lead to your home catching fire, such as lightning or a fire in a neighbouring house spreading to yours, but the vast majority of domestic fires start inside the home. You can prevent this from happening to you.

So what is fire? Fire is one of those things which we first discover as our perception develops when we are children. At first, this perception is limited in its scope. You must not play with matches because they are dangerous. You must not touch the cooker because it is hot. And you must not stick things into the electric heater because they will start a fire.

As we grow older our understanding of the physical properties of fire as both a benefit and a danger increases, but sadly the chemical explanation of heat and fire given in our school lessons tends to be passed over and forgotten.

Fire is simply a chemical reaction. Without understanding the technicalities, we do understand this basic fact when we light a coal fire in our fireplace. We supply the energy necessary to start the reaction with firelighters or kindling, and supply the ingredients of the reaction with fuel and oxygen.

Fire is invariably a reaction of this sort; fuel, heat and oxygen present in the correct proportions. This reaction is correctly called 'oxidation' or 'combustion'. When oxidation occurs, it will continue for as long as the three ingredients of heat, fuel and oxygen are available. This is because fire is a continuous or 'chain' reaction. Only if one of these ingredients is removed will the reaction cease.

When fighting a fire we try to break the chain at one of these three points. Referring to a fire 'burning itself out' means that the fuel has been exhausted or removed. The fuel is essential to the reaction, as are the heat and the oxygen, so the reaction peters out without it. Sometimes this is done deliberately.

45

Forest plantations usually have carefully organised 'fire breaks'. These are strips or roadways where there are no trees. In the event of a forest fire, the flames would burn until they reached the break and then run out of fuel. If there was a high wind the breaks would not necessarily work, as the flames might jump them, but generally they aid the fire fighter in his work.

In the case of a house fire, however, the fuel is already there. The two main methods of fire fighting are either to remove the heat from the reaction by cooling it with water, or to remove the oxygen by smothering the flames. The latter can be achieved in a variety of ways, including fire blankets or wet tea cloths, or by using a dry powder fire extinguisher.

The different ways of fighting fire in your own home, and the occasions when you should attempt this, are discussed later, but the important point to remember for the time being is the chemical nature of fire. We noted earlier that fire is a chain reaction. The speed at which it burns depends largely upon the supply of fuel and oxygen. The greater the supply of these, then the greater the reaction and the greater the liberation of heat. The greater the heat then the faster and more intense the reaction, and so on.

# The 'two minute fire'

Fire can develop and spread very quickly indeed. In the presence of a well-ventilated supply of highly-combustible fuel, fire is quite capable of spreading faster than a man can run. This can lead to the phenomenon that some experts call the 'two minute fire'. Especially in the present age, where so many household materials and products contain highly-flammable chemicals, it is possible for fire under specific circumstances to spread through a house in little more than two minutes. Try timing that on your watch and imagine how little time it gives you and your family to escape.

The fire at Bradford City's Valley Parade football ground on May 11, 1985 has been mentioned already as a case in which the rapid spread of flames and toxic by-products caused a heavy loss of life. In that particular instance, a good supply of oxygen and toxic fumes from flammable seating and constructional materials, allowed a football stand capable of accommodating between 3,000 and 4,000 people to become an inferno in 3 minutes 23 seconds. By that time, the temperature had become so high (about 1,000 degrees centigrade) that cars parked outside the ground were spontaneously bursting into flames.

Fifty-three people lost their lives in the Bradford fire, yet five fire brigade appliances arrived less than four minutes after the first flames were spotted. After the Manchester Woolworths fire and the Star Dust Disco fire in Ireland, the Fire Research Station at Borehamwood carried out full-scale simulated tests. In both cases they found that the premises became untenable after two minutes.

These are all large structures and environments, so you could expect your own home to be destroyed with similar speed if you allow the correct circumstances to develop.

In the case of the Bradford fire, the analogy with the chemical reaction we discussed earlier was exact and clearly visible. The reaction began with loose, easily-combustible kindling beneath the seats; the wooden stand provided a good source of fuel for the reaction, and a breeze supplied a rich source of oxygen. The result was a fire that moved so quickly that some experienced fire fighters likened it to a 'crown fire', a forestry term for a fire that spreads from tree top to tree top.

# The spread of fire inside the home

It is always dangerous to talk in general terms about any subject, including the development and spread of a fire in your home, but the imagination needs some form of model before it can picture such a catastrophe in a familiar environment, enabling you to take suitable steps to prevent its occurrence.

Fire will normally have four fairly distinct phases: incipient, smouldering, flame and heat. At the earliest or 'incipient' stage, there may be no visible evidence of fire at all. Typical examples might include a lighted cigarette end in a wastepaper basket, an electrical fault in a television set, or a spark from an open fire.

If the fuel is there to feed it, the source of the reaction will begin to smoulder. There will still be little or no evidence of flames, but smoke will be visible. The smouldering stage can continue for some time. Even if the supply of fuel and oxygen is good, it may take some time before the temperature required to accelerate the reaction properly has been reached. Once this has occurred, flames will be seen and the reaction will start in full.

Sometimes, of course, the first two stages might be bypassed. Typical examples of this include a chip pan that bursts into flames or an aerosol that is ignited. However, fires of this sort do not usually lead to fatalities. In 1984 fires involving cooking appliances were the most frequent, yet caused only 5 per cent of the fatal casualties.

Once the flames have appeared, they will start rising from their original source towards the ceiling and spreading sideways across the floor. Furniture will by now have started to discolour and smoke production will be increasing, carrying with it particles of unburnt fuel. The air temperature in the room is uncertain, but will probably be hot enough to boil water. There will be an exchange between the interior and exterior, as cool air is drawn inwards to feed the fire, and heat, fumes and smoke escape to other areas of the home.

**At a certain temperature the air becomes superheated, and 'flashover' occurs. This means that portions of the room not in contact with the flames can still be ignited purely by the heat of the air. The effect of this is that the room will appear completely engulfed in flames in a matter of seconds. Prior to flashover objects in the room were absorbing heat, after it they will be radiating heat.**

Inside the room, all but the lower few feet of the air space will have filled with smoke; outside the room smoke and fumes will be filtering throughout the house. The temperature inside will now be so great that it would cook the lungs of anybody who breathed it and the atmosphere will contain deadly poisonous fumes such as carbon monoxide and hydrogen cyanide. If the door of the room fits well and is closed, the fire and heat will be contained in the room for some time. Contrary to popular impressions, wood is actually quite good from a structural point of view in a fire – hence the blackened timbers still left standing after many buildings have been gutted.

If the door is open, or is opened whilst the room is burning, then the heat and flames may be able to spread rapidly throughout the rest of the house. Although this is a point which will be examined later, it is important to note now that if you suspect that a room in your house is on fire you must not open the door to check, but should evacuate your home as quickly as possible and call the fire brigade.

Wooden doors are a simple and surprisingly effective method of containing fire. We have mentioned already that, of the 101,500 fires which occurred in occupied buildings during 1984, 92,100 (91 per cent) were confined to the room of origin. Be aware of this fact. Whether it is when you are doing your nightly check before going to bed, or when you suspect you have a room on fire and feel inclined to investigate, close all doors and keep them closed.

# How fire can kill or injure

It might seem pointless or even a little morbid to examine a question such as this; we all know that if we come into contact with something hot it burns us and that if we come into contact with an excess of heat it can burn us to death. This is certainly a true observation, but it by no means fully explains the dangers of fire in our environment, nor the precautions that should be taken to avoid them.

Emphasis must always be placed on prevention, and much of the later part of this section examines ways of preventing a fire from occurring in the first place. However, the unpleasant reality is that fires do start in houses and will continue to do so.

Throughout 1984, a total of 887 people lost their lives in fires in the United Kingdom, one of the lowest figures for some years. Of these people, only 262 were killed by burns whereas 553 were killed by being overcome by smoke or gases. In some cases the victim was overcome by fumes before being burned, but the vast majority died as the result of the fumes themselves. So whilst it is true to say that fire is dangerous because it burns you, we must qualify this by saying that fire is even more dangerous because it unleashes poisonous gases and fumes.

In the days before foam-plastic furniture fillings and coverings, experienced firemen would often pride themselves on their ability to 'chew' air out of smoke. Where the source of the fire was natural, such as wood or horsehair, the smoke that came off it would be largely composed of particles of ash and carbon suspended in the air heated by the flames. By masticating a mouthful of this smoke, the ash could be removed from the air, and the fireman would be able to stand exposure to the smoke for a short period without breathing equipment.

**These days the smoke will often contain poisonous gases given off by the plastics that fill so many of our homes. Firemen need full breathing apparatus before they can enter many burning buildings and any occupant trapped inside may be quickly overcome and killed by fumes like hydrogen cyanide.**

So the two main threats posed by fire are the obvious one of the flames themselves, and the less obvious one of the fumes given off by them.

Whilst it is easy to stress the dangers of fire and to highlight the number of people killed by fire in the home every year, it is important also to emphasise the much, much higher number of people who escape without injury, or who are only slightly injured.

During 1984 non-fatal casualties outnumbered fatal casualties by twelve to one. There were also a total of 7,350 rescues from fires, of which 3,290 were undertaken by the fire brigade, and 4,060 without any assistance. If sensible precautions are taken to prevent fire breaking out in the first place, and to help ease of escape if it does, then the likelihood of you or your family suffering serious injury is greatly reduced.

# Toxic and flammable materials

We mentioned above that most of the people who are killed in domestic fires are not killed by the flames themselves, but are overcome by the toxic fumes and gases that they give off. Naturally, most materials that burn will give off smoke and in a sufficiently great concentration this smoke will 'asphyxiate' (suffocate – see p.180). This means that the smoke and carbon monoxide will prevent oxygen from reaching your lungs and thus prevent your vital organs from functioning.

With some materials, however, combustion will release not only smoke and carbon monoxide, but toxic fumes such as hydrogen cyanide as well. These fumes are by-products of the chemical reaction and will sometimes overcome and kill somebody within a matter of seconds. Whereas smoke has to be fairly dense to overcome someone, toxic fumes of the sort given off by, for instance, PVC (polyvinyl chloride) can achieve the same or even worse effects in less time and with lower concentrations.

## Furniture

It is an unfortunate fact that some fire victims unconsciously design their own deaths into their environments. Certain types of synthetic (man-made) materials are identified as being capable of releasing toxic fumes when they burn. These are used primarily for the stuffings of furniture, toys and such like. It is up to you to ensure either that you do not buy furniture containing these materials, or that you only buy it if it has been treated to reduce its flammability. Laws exist to help you in this.

Particular materials give off particular by-products when they burn. Wood and paper produce acrolein, polyurethane foam (often used as stuffing) gives off cyanides (including hydrogen cyanide), and PVC produces hydrogen chloride.

Chief Fire Officers have pointed out that one three-piece suite on fire is capable of completely filling a room with smoke (at the 'flame' stage of a fire) within three minutes. For that

51

matter, just one centimetre of the PVC insulation used on electric cables is capable of filling a one-litre bottle with deadly hydrogen chloride gas.

Ideally, one would prefer to return to the days when chemicals of this sort were not in common usage without losing any of the benefits of modern technology, but this is impossible. The example of the PVC insulation shows that a television set, hi-fi or, for that matter, any other electrical appliance contains sufficient PVC to produce masses of toxic fumes. This is not likely to change. Nor are we likely to start stuffing our furniture with horsehair again.

However, we can try to identify the main areas of concern, and select items that are flame proofed when we purchase, for instance, some new furniture. If the outer covering or upholstery of an armchair will not itself burn, then this delays considerably the point at which any synthetic stuffing can begin to produce toxic gases.

It was for this reason that legislation was introduced to control the flammability of upholstered furniture. The three main areas of legislation that are of interest here are: The Upholstered Furniture (Safety) Regulations 1980, The Upholstered Furniture (Safety) (Amendment) Regulations 1983, and The Children's Furniture (Safety) Order 1982.

Every year fires which start in upholstered furniture kill about 160 people and injure a further 1,000. Approximately two-thirds of these fires are caused by smokers' materials such as cigarette ends, cigars, sparks, matches, and lighted pipes. Putting this into perspective, the figures mean that approximately 23 per cent of domestic fire fatalities and 13 per cent of non-fatal casualties are caused by fires of this type.

The regulations were introduced to reduce these risks and to increase public awareness of the dangers. Apart from the regulations on children's furniture, they apply to all upholstered furniture designed or suitable for use in the home, including furniture intended to be assembled after it has been supplied. They do not, however, apply to furniture designed or intended for use wholly or mainly as a bed, music stools, small stools or pouffes, furniture designed or intended for use wholly or mainly out of doors, furniture suitable for use by children under the age of 11 years, second-hand furniture,

furniture without an upholstered seat (provided the seat is not in contact with any upholstered arms or back), furniture intended for export, and bespoke (made-to-order) furniture.

The furniture covered by these regulations must be subject to the flammability tests of BS 5852 part 1. In this, the materials of which the furniture is made (especially the upholstery and filling) are subjected to two tests. In the first a smouldering cigarette end is placed in the frame at the joint between the back and the seat. In the second a small butane gas flame is used to simulate a lighted match. If the material used by the manufacturer would normally be flammable, but has been given a flame-retardant treatment, then the material is first washed to check that the treatment is water-fast.

## Children's furniture

Children's furniture is subjected to similar tests under BS 5852 part 2, but these use a somewhat stronger ignition source. If the furniture passes these safety checks, and only if it passes them, then it can carry a square safety display label informing you of that fact. This shows a picture of a lighted cigarette and match with the word 'resistant' on one side, and the words 'Meets the requirements for resistance to cigarette and match ignition in the Upholstered Furniture (Safety) Regulations' on the other side.

If, however, the furniture failed either or both of the tests then it must display a triangular label warning you of that fact, with a picture of either (or both) a cigarette or a match on one side and the words 'Careless use of cigarettes and matches could set fire to this furniture' on the other.

Also, furniture that fails either or both of these tests must carry a permanent label telling you this. The label should be fixed in such a way that it can be seen when the item is tilted at right-angles to its normal position.

As a general principle, buy furniture that complies with these regulations. Do not hesitate to press any shopkeeper or assistant if they do not know off-hand whether an article of furniture complies or not. If necessary, insist that they contact the manufacturer or supplier to find out for you, but bear in mind that furniture supplied by a reputable manufacturer would comply with the legal requirement to display labels.

## Checking flammability

It is a good idea to be your own inspector after buying potentially flammable articles. Cut off a small section from an unseen hem or part of the item and subject it to heat from matches or a cigarette lighter. You can also obtain samples of the stuffing of soft toys, bedding or furniture by cutting a few stitches in one of the less-visible seams. Non-flammable or flame-retardant materials will char or melt, but will not easily burn. Untreated flammable materials, however, will often burst into flames with surprising vigour. Ensure that you do not carry out this kind of experiment in an enclosed area or near other flammable materials.

# Fire fighting

Highly-trained professional people exist to fight fire on your behalf. A percentage of people, more often men than women (see p.62) are injured or killed every year because they unwisely attempt to fight fire in their home or workplace. Except on any occasion where you can catch a fire at its point of ignition, you should evacuate your house as soon as possible and call the fire brigade. There are certain types of safety and fire fighting equipment that will help you to do this, which are examined in detail below, but it is important that you use these correctly.

A typical domestic fire extinguisher (dry powder, 1 Kg weight) could save your life or the life of a member of your family if you use it, for instance, to extinguish any flames blocking an exit route. But you must not overestimate its potential. An extinguisher like that would be practically useless if an entire room was on fire and would be positively dangerous if you allowed it to give you the confidence to tackle such a fire. Instead, call the fire brigade.

## *Fire brigade*

After a Joint Committee of the Central Fire Brigades Advisory Council's recommendation in 1958 almost every populated area in Britain has been divided into four main risk categories. These categories (A, B, C and D) determine the minimum weight of attack that the brigade should dispatch to an emergency call. That is, the number of appliances and the time within which they should arrive.

**For your own fire safety, ascertain which risk category your house belongs to.**

Category 'A' risk areas are normally only found in the largest cities and towns. These will be of a substantial size and contain a lot of buildings where there is a high risk of fire that would cause considerable loss of life or property damage. Category 'A' risks could include areas of large, densely-populated buildings and industries that use flammable or dangerous chemicals. If a fire station receives an emergency call from a category 'A' risk area it must have two appliances at the scene within five minutes and a third there within eight minutes of the original call.

Category 'B' risk areas are also found in the largest cities and towns and include continuously built-up areas that present a high risk of lost lives or property in the event of a fire, but which are not covered by a Category 'A' risk area. The response to a 'B' risk call would be one appliance arriving within five minutes and a second within eight minutes of the original call.

Category 'C' risk areas include the suburbs of large cities, and built-up areas of smaller towns. The minimum recommended response is one appliance within eight to ten minutes, although most of the large brigades have a policy of sending two appliances.

Category 'D' risk areas basically cover all areas not covered by categories A, B and C. The response is one appliance within twenty minutes.

Remote buildings in the countryside sometimes fall within a separate category where the weight of attack is at the operational discretion of the Chief Fire Officer. If you are worried that you might fall into this category, telephone your local fire brigade and ask them what their response would be if your building caught fire. If you have any worries about the time that it would take them to get to you, ask if their Fire Prevention Officer (FPO) would call at your house and advise you about any special precautions you might take against the possibility of fire breaking out.

Wherever you live, your local fire brigade will be able to tell you both the risk category area that your house falls in, their response to calls in that area (which may be higher than the minimum recommendation), and whether they have a fire prevention advisory service. You will probably find that your local station will have an FPO who can discuss the fire safety of your house with you.

If a fire does start in your house do not hesitate to dial 999 and ask for the fire brigade. Some authorities have suggested that you should memorise how to dial 999 with your eyes closed to simulate darkness or smoke. This is a good idea in so far as that you might become trapped in your house, or inside a room with a telephone, but for goodness' sake do not consider entering or waiting in smoke-filled rooms to call the fire brigade; escape as quickly as possible and call them from a neighbour's house or public phone box. Be sure to give your address in full and if possible give them some local landmark for guidance.

## Extinguishing small fires

Providing that you have suitable equipment (see p.62) you can tackle small fires at their point of ignition. Typical causes of fire include: chip pan or frying pan fires, upholstery, clothing (see p.188 for advice on this), portable heaters and electrical equipment. Always remember to keep escape routes clear and never position yourself with the source of fire between you and the exit from the room. Also, instigate a precautionary evacuation of the house, avoid breathing any fumes and direct fire extinguishers or water at the base of the flames. Do not panic and discharge a domestic fire extinguisher indiscriminately, as it will quickly empty.

## Chip pans

Cooking appliances cause the greatest number of domestic fires in the United Kingdom and approximately 80 per cent of these are started by fat or cooking oil. If it is possible for you to approach the cooker safely, turn off the heat source. You must never attempt to carry or move a burning chip pan or frying pan, as you would run the risk of the fat spilling out. This could both burn you and help the fire to spread. Furthermore, you must never use water or a fire extinguisher to put the flames out. Burning fat or oil will float on the surface of water and both the force of a fire extinguisher or thrown water would spatter hot and burning oil from the pan. Instead, swiftly soak a towel or tea cloth in water. Hold the cloth as a shield in front of you and approach the fire. Place the towel over the pan to smother the flames. Ideally, you will have a fire blanket near the cooker to do this with (see p.64). A close-fitting lid or plate would also do the job, but these would not protect your arms and hands from the flames.

**Once the fire is extinguished, leave the cover on for at least 30 minutes. Fat and oil retain their heat for a long time and may reignite if the cover is removed too soon. If you have not already turned the heat source off, do so now.**

## Furniture

Remembering the risks associated with synthetic upholstery materials, take no risks with furniture fires. Water is the best extinguishant to use as it cools the heat effectively, though others could be used (see p.63). Completely smother the item with your extinguisher. If you are not using a water-based fire extinguisher, then follow up your initial attack with buckets of water to completely soak the stuffing. Once the fire is out, allow the item time to cool down and then remove it from the building.

In such cases, always keep an escape route clear. Apart from somebody capable of filling buckets with water for you, ask everyone else to leave the house. Synthetic fabrics and materials have a tendency to 'flare up' suddenly and burn with an intense heat. Do not stand close to them and avoid breathing any fumes.

## Gas and oil

Oil heaters on fire may result in a spillage of burning liquids, so water-based extinguishers should not be used. Do not try to carry the heater to safety, but use an appropriate extinguisher (such as dry powder) directed through the ventilation slots if the fire is inside, or at the base of any visible flames.

Liquefied Petroleum Gas (LPG) involves its own special hazards, including the risk of the bottle exploding. If you can safely turn off the gas supply at the bottle, do so. If you cannot do this, evacuate the building immediately and call the fire brigade. Tell them that bottled gas is involved. In the unlikely event of a domestic gas supply igniting, evacuate the home immediately and call the fire brigade.

## Electrical equipment

Electrical faults are the cause of many domestic fires. If an appliance catches fire try to unplug it at the power point if possible. During daylight hours this can be done by switching off the power at your mains fuse panel.

**Foam or water-based extinguishers must not be used on an electrical fire unless the power has been switched off. With apparatus such as television sets, where quite high voltages are retained after the set has been switched off, water or foam extinguishers must never be used.**

With fires in television sets, do not approach the set as the tube could implode with the heat. Call the fire brigade. Avoid breathing any fumes or smoke as these will be extremely toxic. Do not open windows to clear the air. Some authorities recommend throwing a wet blanket over the set to contain both flying glass and the spread of the flames, although you should only do this if the power has been disconnected. Do not look under any such cover, but leave the house and wait for the fire brigade to arrive.

Electric blankets occasionally overheat and cause fires. If this happens, do not open the window to clear the fumes nor roll back the blankets to inspect the damage. Unplug the blanket at the wall and call the fire brigade. If it is safe to do so, you can then drench the bed with water.

# Escaping from a fire

Fighting fire at its point of ignition is all very well when it is possible, but domestic fires often develop through the night when the occupants of the house are asleep. We have already established that, whilst sources of sudden ignition (such as cooking fat) account for the greatest number of domestic fires, it is the slow, smouldering sources (such as electrical faults or cigarette ends) which cause the most deaths. Indeed, we could take a cigarette end dropped carelessly down the back of an armchair covered with flammable upholstery as a typical example. This is most likely to happen late at night when you are feeling tired. Whilst the armchair, once alight, could flare and spread to the rest of the room very rapidly, the 'smouldering' stage could continue for some time before reaching the temperature necessary to ignite the upholstery. During the interim period, you might have gone to bed and fallen asleep. The first you would know of the fire would be when it was far too late for you to fight it. Escape from the building would be the only possible action under such circumstances.

In the event of a fire like this, your reaction will probably be one of panic. This is not necessarily bad or abnormal in itself, since the traditional view that evacuations should be carried out in an orderly and panic-free manner has on occasions contributed to events that have cost people their lives. The simple fact is that many modern buildings and interior materials do not allow people much time before they ignite and release toxic chemicals into the atmosphere. In 1977 a fire at the Kentucky Beverley Hills Supper Club in the United States killed 164 people. Subsequent investigations by Kentucky State and the National Fire Protection Association attributed the cause partly to the fact that there was a delay before people were informed of the existence of the fire and partly to a failure to appreciate its seriousness. While access to the escape exits was still possible, there was no panic. When the escape routes had gone, it is presumed that there was panic.

Whereas panic itself is not desirable, an acute sense of urgency certainly is valuable. The best way to avoid panic in such a situation is to have a clear sense of your intended response to a domestic fire before it occurs. And the best way to achieve this is to pre-plan an escape route.

## Escape routes

Walk around your house and imagine how you would reach safety from each room should its exit be blocked by fire. Try to plan the best route out in such an event and an alternative should that one be blocked. Remember that it would probably be dark and ask yourself how easy it would then be to follow the route. Are there handrails or balustrades that you could follow? Are there any flights of steps that could easily be fallen down? These are the basic questions that need to be answered when you plan your escape route.

Remember that a fire is most likely to start downstairs. Examine your upstairs rooms and ask yourself which of them would be difficult both for you to escape from and for the fire brigade to effect a rescue from. These rooms may well benefit from a rope-ladder, knotted rope or wall-fixed fire escape. If you do use such a device, ensure that everybody knows how it functions and that it is well secured inside; it would be self-defeating for somebody to use a knotted rope to escape from a burning building only to injure themselves with a fall from an improperly secured fixing. Check that no rooms have windows which are difficult for you or your children to open. Remember that your children are smaller and weaker than you.

**Double glazing can sometimes be particularly difficult to open. If necessary, position hammers, mallets or lengths of wood near the window so that anybody trapped behind it could break their way out in an emergency.**

## Fire drills

It is a good idea to draw up a fire drill for you and your family.

Practise this, with an assembly point outside. Treat such a drill seriously and use it as an opportunity to identify potential problems before they occur.

If you discover a fire, shut the door of the room immediately. If the door is closed and feels hot, or if smoke is coming around the edges of it, do not open it. Raise the alarm with anybody else in the building. Having a fire-alarm system fitted is neither impossible nor especially expensive. On the other hand, even the old-fashioned hand-held school bell can prove quite adequate in the average home.

**Make sure that everybody in the home is awake and actively escaping. Do not forget that whilst adults will probably make their own escape sensibly and quickly, your children may well think of safety as being a matter of finding you.**

Call the fire brigade as soon as possible. If anybody is trapped in the building, tell the brigade this. As we have already said, do not take any risks attempting to call the brigade – use a neighbour's telephone or public telephone box. You must not enter the building after you have left it unless you have been told by the fire brigade that it is safe to do so. If you are trapped on the upper floor, crawl to the front rooms where you can be seen by people outside. Crawling on the floor is important because any smoke or fumes, being hot, will rise. The few feet just above the floor are those most likely to be free of smoke.

If any of your doors open on to a communal staircase, then these should, by law, be fire-resistant and self-closing. If you are going to rent or buy a flat, remember that it should be designed so that you do not have to pass through a living room or kitchen to get from the bedroom to the exit door.

One final note of caution. Psychological studies of human behaviour have shown a surprisingly high degree of willing-ness amongst members of the public to fight fire. These studies used sample cases where the fire brigade had to attend and ultimately had to extinguish the fire. In the cases studied, the people concerned believed that it was within their capabilities to extinguish the fire – one conclusion of which is that our ability to judge the severity of a fire is not good. The same research showed that untrained people were twice as likely to tackle a fire at work as they were at home. One of the reasons for this might simply be that their workplace is more likely to contain the tools of fire fighting: extinguishers, hoses, and so on. This in itself is an argument for caution and restraint with any equipment that you buy for domestic use.

**Men between the ages of 20 and 39 are the most likely to re-enter a burning building, especially if they know the building well, have previously been involved in a fire, and if the fire in question is producing smoke. Resist any such instincts.**

# Fire extinguishers

We have already mentioned that domestic fire extinguishers may be of doubtful value. Sometimes they are criticised for being either too heavy for easy handling, or too small for effective use. The smaller ones (1 kg or less) will discharge quickly and a nervous, panic-stricken householder might discharge a small fire extinguisher without even aiming it at the fire, thus wasting time that could have been spent calling for the fire brigade. And, of course, fire extinguishers are dangerous if used on fires such as chip pans.

However, having emphasised their negative points, it is nevertheless clear that fire extinguishers in the home can serve a useful function. All too often a fire can start from a small and easily-extinguishable source – perhaps a tea cloth that is ignited by the hot ring of a cooker. Under such circumstances many people find themselves in the unenviable position of watching a more serious fire develop and not having anything to fight it with.

Providing that you understand that the above example is practically the limit of most domestic fire extinguishers, then you may find them a useful investment. Although fire brigade research shows that in cases where fires were extinguished before their arrival, buckets of water, hosepipes and fire blankets often proved more useful than extinguishers, you may be confronted with fires (such as electrical fires) where such methods would be inappropriate.

Fire extinguishers should conform to BS 5423, except for the small aerosol type sold for cars, which should conform to BS 6165. Look also for a BS Kitemark, or a BAFE (British Approvals for Fire Equipment) or FOC (Fire Offices' Committee) approval mark.

Different extinguishers are suitable for different types of fire. In general, fire types are divided into three classes: A (burning materials like furniture, cloth or wood), B (burning liquids such as oil), and C (burning gases). Class C fires do not fall within the normal expectations of the domestic fire fighter, so it is the A and B ratings that are most relevant. The extinguisher should have a class rating printed on it. This will be accompanied by a number to indicate the size of fire it is capable of fighting. For instance, an extinguisher marked 21B is capable of extinguishing a larger area of burning oil than one that is marked 13B. In general, an extinguisher for use in the home should have a rating of not less than both 8A and 21B.

## Types of extinguisher

In addition, the extinguisher can contain one of five different extinguishants. These all have their advantages and disadvantages.

**Water:** Water extinguishers have the advantage of cooling a fire efficiently, thus reducing the chances of reignition. They are, however, heavy and are only suitable for class A fires. They are also unsuitable for electrical fires. Extinguishers containing water should be coloured red, or have a red label.

**Multi-purpose foam:** This is suitable for both class A and B fires, and cools efficiently. It is unsuitable, however, for electrical fires. Extinguishers containing foam should be cream in colour.

**Dry powder:** Dry powder is suitable for both A and B fires and is safe on live electrical appliances. The only disadvantages are that it can be difficult to clean up and does not cool very well. Dry powder extinguishers should be coloured blue.

**Carbon dioxide ($CO_2$):** This is exceptionally useful for extinguishing burning liquids and is safe for use on electrical fires. It does not cool very well and may affect the user in confined spaces. The extinguisher should be coloured black.

**Halon (BCF):** Halon is useful on burning liquids, small fires of solid materials, electrical fires, and is clean. However, it has limited capabilities on solid material fires and the agent (BCF) can cause nervous disorders in confined spaces if it reaches a concentration of 5 per cent or more. The extinguisher should be coloured green.

Of these, dry powder is probably the best choice for the domestic user. Ensure that you buy one capable of fighting at least 8A and 21B fires (weight – around 1 kg), and that you have it properly and regularly serviced or replaced. Do not partially discharge it to see whether it still works, and get it recharged after use on a fire, even if you only use a little of its contents. BAFE (48a Eden Street, Kingston-upon-Thames, Surrey KT1 1EE) will be able to send you a list of approved engineers to do this for you.

Positioning fire extinguishers around the house is largely a matter for your own discretion, but choose somewhere generally accessible, such as your hall, and fix the extinguisher prominently. Do not store it in a cupboard, or anywhere out of sight.

One final point: fire extinguishers can be difficult to buy in the High Street, with the result that people tend to settle for models that do not satisfy their needs, or were meant for different purposes such as cars. The best way for you to find someone who stocks what you require is to look under 'Fire' and 'Safety' equipment in your local Yellow Pages.

# Fire blankets

These provide the best way of extinguishing chip pan or frying pan fires and should be wall-mounted in the kitchen. Avoid fixing them right next to the cooker where the heat and smoke could be quite intense in the event of a fire.

Fire blankets are made of a flame-proof cloth capable of smothering the flames on a number of burning materials including, incidentally, clothing. Purchase blankets that meet the requirements of the new BS 6575, which covers suitability for burning liquids and fuels (such as petrol). Cheaper blankets tend to be made of glass-fibre, which is not always reliable – sometimes flaws in the fabric prevent them from functioning fully.

Domestic blankets are usually three feet square, which is quite adequate for chip pan fires and other similar emergencies. It is, however, possible to buy blankets that are four feet square. This extra size is useful if you ever need to wrap someone up to smother burning clothing, but in general the smaller size should be sufficient for your needs.

Fire blankets are the best things to extinguish chip pan fires

## Smoke detectors

Throughout this section we have repeatedly emphasised that

65

speed is essential in discovering a fire and evacuating your house. The longer that a fire burns the more likely it is to cause fatalities or injuries.

Amongst some people smoke detectors gained an unfortunate reputation as items of electronic 'gimmickry' when they were introduced, with the result that they are not widely fitted in this country. In the United States, however, their use is widely accepted, and with excellent results. Now Chief Fire Officers in this country are calling for more people to fit them in their homes. Whilst no form of early-detection system will compensate for a lack of precautions to prevent fire starting, smoke detectors are a sensible buy and highly recommended. They are also cheap and can be fitted by the average handyman.

## Types of detector

Detectors use one of two mechanisms: ionisation or photoelectric detection. In the first a small radioactive source ionises the air within the detector. This produces ions (electrically-charged particles) and allows a small current to flow from a battery. The alarm is triggered if smoke enters the detector and reduces the current flow. In the second type smoke scatters a small light beam and activates a photoelectric detector. Research has tended to suggest that the ionisation type is better at detecting heat (i.e. from a well-established fire), whilst the photoelectric type is better at detecting a smouldering fire.

Detectors come in small plastic casings which can be fitted to interior surfaces. Remembering that smoke and heat rise, they should be fitted on the ceiling, with one in the downstairs hall. Another one fitted to the ceiling of the upstairs landing would also detect bedroom fires.

When they sense a fire detectors emit a loud alarm. They are powered by 9 V batteries and usually have a variety of test systems to check that the battery, alarm and detector are all functioning. You must follow the manufacturer's recommendations when buying new batteries. Certain types can be interconnected to form a system so that if one alarm goes off, they all do. It might be a good idea to fit them in every room where you suspect there is a fire risk as doors properly closed at night can delay the escape of fire and thus delay the functioning of the alarm.

False alarms are the only drawback with smoke detectors, but over-sensitive devices are far preferable to under-sensitive ones. False alarms can be caused by sudden draughts or by the detector being fitted too close to the kitchen.

Both ionisation and photoelectric detectors are known as 'point-type' and should conform to BS 5445 part 7. This outlines the requirements, test methods, and performance criteria for resettable smoke detectors.

# General precautions

As part of your daily routine, you can take precautions to limit the possibility of fire breaking out in the first place, and to contain its spread should it do so.

## Flammable materials

We have already talked in passing about the flammability of materials used within your home and steps that can be taken to avoid using them for certain purposes. But the fact is that you will not be able to avoid flammable materials altogether. For instance, many soft toys and articles of children's wear made by reputable manufacturers will have flammable covering. Sadly, this will probably not be illegal. However, if you make the effort to identify those things in your home that are flammable and to segregate them from possible sources of ignition, then you can minimise any risk that they pose.

Look out especially for DIY materials used to improve the home. Ceiling coverings such as polystyrene tiles can be a hazard if they are fitted with insufficient adhesive or painted with gloss paint. Wall tapestries should be tested for flammability; use the 'scissors' test, snipping a little of the fabric from the back or edge and subjecting it to direct heat from a match, cigarette lighter or blow torch.

**Whilst wood can be structurally quite resistant to fire, light, dry softwoods can be highly flammable, especially if they have been treated with certain paints or lacquers. Wooden cladding may require some form of fire protection such as fire-resistant varnish – consult your DIY supplier for advice.**

Avoid building bonfires in your own home! Unintentionally, people often construct almost tailor–made pyres in odd corners of their houses. Piles of old newspapers, clothes, rubbish and DIY materials are just waiting for the spark they need to catch fire – hunt them out and clean them up before this occurs. Particular areas of danger include under-stairs cupboards. The stairwell can act as a chimney if fire breaks out. Any rags that have been used to wipe spirits such as turpentine substitute (white spirit) can spontaneously ignite if they are left crumpled up. Make sure that any such rags are removed from the house after use.

## Smokers

Smokers cause the highest number of serious domestic fires every year, so particularly repressive safety rules need to be applied! Beware of balancing acts with lighted cigarettes on the edges of objects or furniture. Make sure that cigarettes are stubbed out carefully in ashtrays and that matches are completely dead before being discarded. Avoid smoking in the bedroom, or when you are feeling tired or intoxicated – these are all recurrent themes in fatal fires caused by smokers. Also, make checking your furniture part of your nightly routine. Run your hands round the back and sides of armchairs to make doubly sure that no cigarette ends have fallen down them. Fluff-up and turn over cushions as well. Avoid emptying ashtrays into wastepaper bins last thing at night.

One good tip to follow with any room that has an identifiable spark or fire risk, whether it be from smokers or an open fire, is to turn off all the lights and stand in the dark for a few seconds. This improves your chances of spotting any smouldering or loose sparks.

## Nightly fire safety check

You should, without fail, follow a routine nightly check before you go to bed. In addition to the precautions mentioned above, switch off and unplug all electric appliances in every room. Switch off lights and close all doors. In particular, check that the television set has been switched off and unplugged and that all gas and electric cooker rings and burners are completely off. Make sure that there is nothing hanging over central heating radiators and be especially careful with oil-filled electric radiators. As these do not have a visible heat source it is tempting to hang wet clothes on them to dry out. This prevents the radiator from heating the room properly. The thermostat may consequently fail to operate correctly, with the resultant danger of over-heating.

## Open fires and oil heaters

Open fires of any type should be protected by a fireguard or, in the case of wood or coal fires, a sparkguard. These are both to prevent things from falling into the fire and to prevent the fire from spitting sparks on to anything that could burn.

Sparkguards for coal fires should conform to BS 3248. Fireguards attached to electric, gas or oil heaters should conform to BS 1945, and safety fireguards (rather than sparkguards) for use with solid fuel appliances should conform to BS 6539.

Paraffin heaters have the advantage of being cheap and efficient, but they are potentially dangerous and should be treated with respect. Always fill the heaters outside and snuff or blow them out some time before going to bed, checking them once more before retiring.

With upright heaters, the top can become so hot that the air rising from it will be capable of igniting a match. Be especially careful to ensure that heaters of this sort are protected with a fireguard and are not put in such a position that anybody could fall over them. Some insurance policies, usually cheaper ones catering for a number of properties simultaneously, will exclude oil heaters. It may be that you should check this.

Remember also that un-flued oil and paraffin heaters emit noxious fumes, so ensure that the room in which you use them is well ventilated.

If you have solid fuel fires, heaters, ovens or central heating systems, you will need to empty the ash every night. Deposit this outside in suitable containers and riddle and clean your fire early in the evening – not a few minutes before you go to bed.

## Electrical fire risks

By and large, these have been covered in other sections, notably 'Electrical safety', 'Fire safety: Open fires and oil heaters' and 'Fire safety: Nightly checks'. However, there are a few remaining points of general concern.

Firstly, we return once more to televisions. It has already been noted that these should be switched off at the wall plug as well as the set, but also try to ensure that they are well segregated from potentially flammable materials, such as loose curtains hanging behind the set, or newspapers left on top. Other general tips include replacing worn or old wiring, ensuring the correct fuse rating and avoiding flexes running under carpets or rugs. Some appliances need to be left on 24 hours a day to fulfil their proper function: fridges, freezers, central heating systems and immersion heaters.

**These electrical appliances must have their wiring double-checked. Ensure the correct fuse rating and cable diameter and make sure that all electrical parts are in good condition.**

If the house is left empty for some time, such as during a holiday, the freezer presents its own special problem: it is impossible to turn the power off at the mains fuse panel without defrosting both it and its contents. The only practical solution other than getting the freezer wired-in independently is to remove all the fuses from the panel except the one for the freezer circuit. Finding the correct fuse is simple. Switch off the mains and remove all the fuses. Put in one fuse and switch the mains back on. If the freezer does not come on (which is usually indicated by a small external light), turn off the mains and put a second fuse in. Repeat this until the correct fuse is found and either mark the carrier or record its position for future reference.

Avoid old fridges or freezers if possible. When fridges are 'reconditioned', this must be done to the very highest professional standards. If in any doubt, have the fridge serviced and checked by a reputable dealer or manufacturer.

Freezers should conform to BS 3999 (10), BS 922 and BS 1961, but these are principally technical specifications relating to the main performance characteristics, measuring and testing methods, construction and production rather than to safety. Electric fridges and freezers should also conform to BS 3456 (3.18). This standard is specifically concerned with safety. Gas fridges and freezers should conform to BS 5258 part 6 which gives the safety requirements and associated test methods for domestic equipment.

Remember to keep the outlet clear on such machines and check that the pilot light functions well. Gas appliances should be fitted with something called an ignition safety valve, which is operated by a bimetallic spring. In essence, this is a strip of two different metals soldered together and curled over or into the pilot light. When heated, the strip attempts to straighten out and thereby opens the safety ignition valve to release gas through the main burners. If the pilot light goes out the strip contracts and shuts the gas off from the main burners. Make sure that all such valves on any gas appliances are in good working condition by extinguishing the pilot light and checking that this prevents the main burner from functioning.

BS 5258 covers the safety requirements of most domestic gas appliances. Part 1 deals with central heating, part 2 with cookers, part 5 with fires, part 8 with combined fires/back boilers, part 12 with decorative log and artificial fuel-effect fires, and part 14 with barbecues.

Central heating must only be installed by expert or qualified people. If you install it yourself be sure to have it inspected before use. BS 5449 is a code of practice for domestic central heating systems and must be followed at all times. Part 1 covers forced circulation hot water systems.

Immersion heaters should ideally be controlled by a thermostat and should conform to BS 3451 (2.21). They are unlikely to be dangerous unless the hot water tank is empty,

71

which is improbable in an empty house – even if a leak occurred the ball-cock valve of the cold water tank would keep supplying water. Nevertheless, immersion heaters should be switched off when the house is empty for any length of time. Quite apart from the safety aspects, this will save the cost of heating water that nobody is going to use!

# CHEMICAL SAFETY

Dangerous chemicals can affect the safety of an individual in three main ways: by poisoning, by corrosive effects on the skin (chemical burns), and by their flammability.

Short-term effects of exposure to hazardous chemicals can include poisoning by inhalation or by ingestion (drinking or eating toxic substances). Many domestic substances are capable of burning the skin on contact and some (such as mercury, which is found in certain thermometers) can penetrate the skin and attack the system internally. Long-term effects can include chronic illness, brain damage, skin diseases (dermatitis) and even death. Other chemicals can create fire or explosion risks if they are stored or used in the house incorrectly.

Accidents involving chemicals are usually the result of ignorance of their properties, sometimes because of laziness, and sometimes because manufacturers have not clearly labelled their products with instructions for use and with appropriate warnings. It must also be noted that dangerous chemicals are sometimes taken deliberately for incidental reasons such as the narcotic effects of solvents (i.e. glue sniffing) or for the dangerous properties themselves (i.e. suicides). Equally, flammable or explosive chemicals are sometimes deliberately misused for experimentation, entertainment or arson.

Chemicals specific to the DIY workshop, craft process or garage are dealt with later (see p.131). The aspects discussed in this section are: dangerous chemicals in the home, medicines and drugs, poisonous plants, and safe disposal of dangerous chemicals.

Accidental poisoning from inhalation or ingestion of dangerous substances caused 2,865 of the accidents reported in the 1984 HASS report, or 2.6 per cent of the total. As might be expected, the vast majority of these accidents (2,254) involved children of four years old or under.

Of the accidents where the location was known, the danger areas highlighted included the dining room (350 cases), the kitchen (480), the bedroom (341) and the bathroom or toilet (155), but this information must be qualified by the fact that in the biggest single category, the location was unknown.

Although poisonings form a low percentage of total non-fatal domestic accidents, and although many of these were not serious, accidental inhalation or ingestion cause a somewhat higher percentage of actual deaths from domestic accidents every year. In the 1984 HASS report they caused 518 (or 11.3 per cent) of the total of 4,592 fatalities.

# Domestic chemicals

## *Toxic hazards*

The fact that as many as an estimated 7,000 children under 15 years old throughout the United Kingdom are treated in hospital because they have taken potentially poisonous domestic chemicals gives a false impression of the situation. Objective studies show that the toxicity of most chemicals found in or around the home is actually quite low. In other words, you or your children would have to take them in large quantities to suffer any serious harm. Indeed, many of the children taken to hospital because they had swallowed or taken domestic chemicals were not poisoned at all in so far as they did not develop any of the symptoms associated with the particular chemical involved.

**Poisons most likely to cause accidents include: turpentine, bleach, rat poison, disinfectant, and alcohol. One study of fatalities amongst children poisoned by non-medicinal and household products isolated the following as hazards: Cresol (Wright's vaporising fluid), caustic soda, phenol (Ibcol disinfectant), soldering flux, alcohol, turpentine, ethylene chlorhydrine, corrosive acid, sodium nitrate and sodium chlorate.**

Accidental poisoning of adults is also a comparatively minor problem. Most of the deaths in England and Wales are caused by alcohol, fumes and gases such as carbon monoxide. With the exception of alcohol, this is somewhat different range of hazards to those that normally confront children.

Of non-fatal adult accidents, the greatest number are caused by liquids, including bleach and disinfectant. Swallowing petrol after syphoning it from the tank of a car is also highlighted in the statistics. This practice is dangerous and should always be avoided – even if the liquid is not swallowed, its fumes themselves are harmful.

## Preventative measures

Broadly speaking, poisonings involving domestic products fall into two categories: those involving children and those involving adults. With the exception of chemicals that have been decanted into a different bottle, which is a problem encountered by both groups, the causes of the accidents and the precautions necessary to prevent them tend to be different.

In the case of children, poisoning is likely to result from curiosity. Children of a certain age (usually two to three years old) have an almost unquenchable curiosity and will try to take chemicals irrespective of any markings or warnings on their labels. Indeed, they will often see sensible precautions such as child-resistant tops or lids as a challenge to their ingenuity – the British Standard that covers such things (BS 6652) accepts that up to 15 per cent of children will be able to open the top within five minutes.

**Adults are more likely to poison themselves as the result of thoughtlessness or of not reading and properly following the manufacturer's instructions.**

Before looking at the problems of children and adults separately, remember that rule number one for both categories is to avoid storing chemicals or liquids in anything other than their correct container. Storing turpentine, for instance, in an old lemonade bottle is simply inviting a child to take a drink from it. Labelling the replacement bottle is clearly insufficient in itself. Remember that children may be able to recognise a lemonade bottle before they have developed either the ability or the sense of caution to read its label.

**Studies have shown that the greatest number of incidents in which children poison themselves occur when the chemical in question was stored in an unlocked area less than four feet from the ground. Where children are concerned it is doubly important to ensure that all chemicals are kept out of their reach.**

Remember when doing this that adventurous toddlers will often be capable of using chairs or furniture to reach work

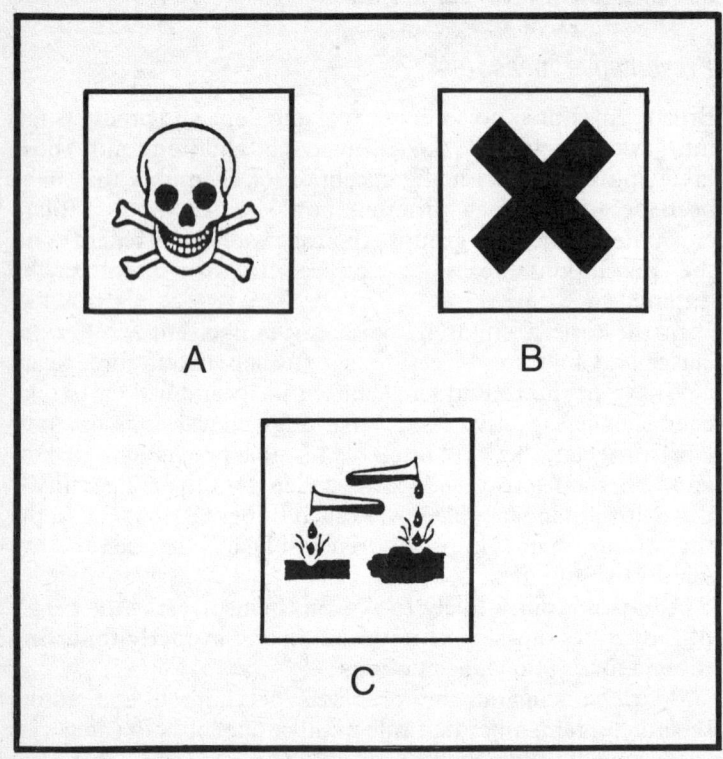

A

B

C

Three common hazard symbols for chemicals
A extremely toxic
B general though limited toxicity
C corrosive

surfaces otherwise out of their range. In these cases the responsibility must always lie with the parent or guardian, both to supervise their children properly and to identify any hazards that household materials might present. Learning how hazards are described by the manufacturer on the label is therefore important.

The Classification, Packaging and Labelling of Dangerous Substances Regulations 1984, require certain hazardous, or potentially hazardous, products to carry a symbol describing their toxic or corrosive properties. This should be accompanied by a word to indicate the severity of the risk. The most familiar of these is the black, diagonal cross against an orange background. This indicates general, although limited, toxicity if the chemical is inhaled, swallowed or allowed to come into contact with the skin and is accompanied by either the word 'Harmful' or, where the danger is very small indeed, 'Irritant' printed below it. More toxic products should be labelled with a skull and crossbones, with the words 'Toxic' or 'Very Toxic' below. These indicate that the product could be extremely dangerous or could even prove fatal. Corrosive substances are indicated by a symbol that shows two test tubes dripping liquid, one dissolving a piece of solid material, the other a human hand.

All potentially dangerous products, including those that are flammable (see p.129) should be kept away from children. Toxic or corrosive products such as acids, pesticides or paint strippers should also be locked up. Storing these on a high shelf in an outbuilding or workshop is always a good idea, but remember that they are only as inaccessible as the key to the door – be sure to keep that out of the reach of children as well.

Where children are around try to select products that have child-resistant lids, but do not rely upon these alone.

Be careful also to consider the needs of any blind or poor-sighted people likely to come into contact with chemicals that you have in your home. At present, specific poisons (as defined under the Pharmacy and Poisons Act, 1933 and Poisons Act 1972) are required to be sold in bottles with ribbed sides. Medicines for external use which contain any of the thirty or so substances listed by the Medicines (Fluted Bottles) Regulations 1978 and sold in bottles with a capacity of greater than 1.14 litres must also comply with this requirement.

There is not yet any legal requirement for tactile (touch-related) warning symbols on the majority of non-medicinal chemicals. Organisations such as the Royal National Institute for the Blind (RNIB – see the end of the book for the address) should be able to advise you of any special precautions needed.

One final note of warning concerning children: a survey of children over 10 years old who attended hospital for suspected poisoning showed that a staggering 88 per cent (82 out of 93) had taken alcohol, of whom the vast majority were boys. The lesson is obvious!

An important lesson for adults where accidental poisoning is concerned is to read the manufacturer's instructions carefully before using any chemical. The majority of cases where accidental inhalation of toxic fumes causes illness are probably also the result of failing to read warnings or instructions; typical examples where this is important include paint strippers and carbon tetrachloride (dry-cleaning fluid), where adequate ventilation must be ensured.

General precautions for handling potentially-dangerous chemicals include wearing protective clothing (rubber gloves and overalls will be sufficient in most cases), ensuring adequate ventilation (preferably by working out of doors) and preventing environmental contamination.

Areas where contamination must be avoided in particular include living areas, areas where food is prepared, and clothing (hence the importance of overalls). Never eat, drink or smoke in the vicinity of hazardous chemicals or in dusty atmospheres; all of these will increase the chances of accidental ingestion.

If the atmosphere is dusty, it is a good idea to wear a face mask of some description, but note that the 'smog masks' sold in some chemists and DIY shops, which are little more than pads of cotton wool held to the face with an aluminium frame and elastic, are only protection against nuisance dusts and will not offer protection from dangerous materials such as asbestos. See the section on DIY safety for a more detailed description of the types of mask available.

## Pesticides and herbicides

The handling and use of herbicides (such as weedkiller or fungicide) and pesticides (such as rat poison) require the same caution as the handling of other chemicals. Perhaps because such chemicals are self-evidently poisonous the number of accidents caused by them is low.

In total, 106 cases of poisoning were reported in the 1984 HASS report where weedkillers, fungicides, animal and insect poisons, rat and mouse poisons, or mothballs were involved. Of these, rat and mouse poisons caused the greatest number (48 out of 106, or 45 per cent).

More detailed studies by the Royal Society for the Prevention of Accidents (RoSPA) have shown that the majority of cases involved young children (usually one or two years old) who took rat or mouse poison after finding it on the floor or in a cupboard.

Dangerous substances that figure in the statistics include rat and mouse poisons, ant killers, pest killers, paraquat, slug pellets, insecticides and mothballs. Safe storage and careful use of these substances is obviously extremely important. Keep them safely locked away out of the reach of children. Follow the manufacturer's instructions carefully and make sure above all else that traces of the poison are not left around after you have finished using it.

When you buy poisons, try to select the weakest form possible. To a certain extent this will have been done for you under a voluntary agreement, the Pesticides Safety Precautions Scheme, between various government departments, the British Pest Control Association, and others.

In essence, this scheme means that manufacturers and distributors of pesticides have agreed to subject their products to a series of safety requirements although these are not necessarily legally enforceable.

Using the Food and Environment Act 1985, it is likely that the government will shortly introduce new regulations prohibiting the sale of non-approved pesticides.

Avoid improvising with poisons. A typical example of this might include the practice amongst some anglers of killing wasps in their nest to obtain their larvae or grubs for use as bait. Various suggestions about how to 'safely' undertake this hazardous task have been proffered in the angling press over the years, including using potassium cyanide and carbon tetrachloride. Quite apart from the ecological implications of killing many hundreds of pollinating insects, comparatively small quantities of either of these substances can kill people, and quickly. Using them safely requires considerable preparation and professional understanding.

Herbicides and pesticides are covered by the Classification, Packaging and Labelling of Dangerous Substances Regulations and so should have adequate warnings and instructions on them. As with other dangerous chemicals it is important not to decant them into alternative bottles.

If you are using water-carried herbicides such as paraquat, make sure that you do not leave contaminated watering cans or containers lying around. Dispose of all such chemicals thoughtfully (see p.121).

## Medicines and drugs

It is ironic that the most common cause of poisoning in the home is the misuse of substances with a therapeutic purpose. This is perhaps a natural result of treatments which involve the consumption of comparatively strong substances in the form of sweet-like tablets, or palatable liquids.

Although widespread publicity about the dangers of old or unused medicines has unquestionably reduced the number of cases, medicines in general still account for a large proportion of poisonings. An analysis of the 1981-82 HASS report showed that the 20 hospitals surveyed dealt with a total of 1,213 cases in which children under the age of five had taken medicines.

**Particular medicines highlighted include: analgesics, contraceptives, sleeping pills, tranquillisers, vitamin pills and capsules, creams and ointments, and slimming tablets.**

Precautions to protect children include disposing of medicines properly, following prescribed dosages only, never attempting to substitute medicines and keeping all medicines in a locked chest or cabinet. Disposing of old medicines thoughtfully is a sensible thing to do, but you must remember that old medicines do not present the danger that medicines in current use do. Medicines in current use are more likely to be left in an accessible position or left with their top off.

Your local chemist will probably accept old medicines from you and supervise their proper disposal, or will at least advise you of an alternative course of action.

The Pharmaceutical Society of Great Britain has issued guidelines to its members to help promote 'DUMP' (Disposal of Unwanted Medicines) campaigns, including detailed instructions on how to handle drugs brought to them. DUMP campaigns are held from time to time in various parts of the country – your local authority should be able to offer you advice on this.

Whatever you do, be careful not to create hazards by the disposal itself. Do not throw old drugs or medicines away in places where they will be accessible to children, such as domestic wastepaper baskets or bins.

Administering only prescribed dosages of drugs and avoiding substituting one drug for another are fairly self-evident measures to prevent accidental poisoning. If you feel that the dosage or type of drug prescribed for your child is insufficient you must consult your GP. Under no circumstances even consider altering the prescription yourself.

Arguments rage as to whether child resistant lids or individually enclosed 'pop out' strips for tablets or pills are better. Bottles with child resistant closures (CRCs) are unquestionably harder for a child to open, but the British Standard governing them accepts, as mentioned earlier, that a percentage of children will be able to gain access, and once this happens they will have a large number of the pills at their disposal.

With pop out strips covered with a translucent material only one pill would be made available. Experts argue that the novelty of opening the strips would wear off within two or three pills and the extent of any poisoning would therefore be limited.

**On balance, both types have their advantages and disadvantages, with the CRCs coming out slightly on top. But the real point is this: keep all medicines locked up! No**

**child is going to gain access to a good medicine cabinet without a key.**

Two final considerations remain. Firstly, elderly people, who are often absent-minded, can unwittingly leave open bottles of pills in easy reach of visiting children. It is important that they realise the dangers of the pills, and have some arrangement for their storage whilst children are present. Bearing in mind the reasons why they prefer to leave pills out in this way – the bother of locking things in a medicine cabinet and opening bottle lids can be tiresome – one solution might be to keep the pills in a separate, locked room while children are around. Whatever happens, it is sensible for parents or guardians to ask where the pills are when they arrive.

The second point is particularly interesting. Studies have shown that families suffering from certain forms of stress are more likely to experience an accidental poisoning of a child with medicines or drugs. Relevant sources of stress include serious family illness, pregnancy, recent family moves, a parent away from home or one or both parents suffering from depression. Extra diligence will be needed at such times.

Adults present their own problems. It is very difficult to assess how many of the overdoses that occur every year are accidental and how many are suicide or attempted suicide. What is clear, however, is that accidental overdoses are the consequence of not taking sensible precautions such as keeping medicines in their correct container and only taking prescribed doses, and that attempted suicides or suicides imply that dangerous drugs were available at a time of depression. On this last point, the Royal College of Physicians has already recommended that doctors review whether elderly people really need all the drugs they are receiving and whether new prescriptions are really necessary. Everybody else should try to regulate their own dependence on medicines and drugs in a similar way. Avoid taking sleeping pills or tranquillisers if it is possible. Once a course of medicine has finished, dispose of all remaining pills or tablets.

Some medicines can cause side effects such as dizziness, loss of co-ordination and confusion – something that itself can be a cause of accidents. Age Concern publish a booklet – *Know your medicines* which offers practical advice.

## Poisonous plants

Many plants in the garden and countryside can be poisonous and in some cases can prove fatal. As a general rule, never eat any plant unless you are certain of its identity. This is particularly important with fungi, where a spoor impression must be taken before proper identification of many species can be made.

The following is a list of plants where poisoning has been reported. It is by no means exhaustive, but gives a reasonable idea of the number of poisonous plants that exist. Parents can use the identification of poisonous plants as an entertaining and educational outdoor game with their children.

Amaryllis, anemone, *arum maculatum*, Barbados lily, belladonna lily, black bryony, black nightshade, bleeding heart, blood lily, bluebell, box, brooms, buttercups, calico bush, Californian poppy, Cape lily, castor oil plant, chalice vine, Chinaberry, Christmas rose, columbine, cyclamen, daffodil, deadly nightshade, delphinium, dumb cane, egg plant, false acacia, fool's parsley, four o'clock plant, foxglove, fritillary, gladiolus, glory lily, greater celandine, Guernsey lily, hawthorn, heliotrope, herb Paris, holly, horse chestnut, hyacinth, hydrangea, iris, ivy, laburnum, lantea, lily of the valley, lily of the valley tree, lobelia, *lonicera spp*, lupin, menziesia, mezereon, mock orange, monkshood, morning glory, night flowering jessamine, oleander, philodendron, potato, privet, rhododendron, rhubarb, St John's wort, *scilla spp*, snowberry, snowdrops, Solomon's seal, sophora, spindle, spurge laurel, spurges, star of Bethlehem, sweet pea, thorn apple, tiger lily, tobacco, tomato, tulips, Virginia creeper, white hellebore, wisteria, woody nightshade, and yew.

# Other chemical hazards

## Alcohol

Alcohol is a surprisingly common cause of both fatal and non-fatal poisonings in the United Kingdom, and caused 50 deaths between 1982 and 1983. One calculation, based upon the HASS report, estimated that there could have been as many as 5,000 non-fatal poisonings throughout 1984.

Detailed studies of individual fatalities caused by alcohol have shown that the factors involved vary; some people consumed the alcohol at home, others in pubs and yet more at parties. Some cases of both fatal and non-fatal incidents are the result of combining alcohol with drugs, although it is difficult to say how many of these were accidental and how many deliberate.

The only specific advice that can be offered to combat alcohol poisoning relates to youngsters and is confined to the obvious message of close supervision. A more general rule, perhaps, is to avoid taking alcohol with medicines.

It is also worth noting that alcohol causes other accidents: drink driving is perhaps the best publicised form, but others include accidents in the home from trips, slips and falls, and accidents caused by loss of concentration and incapability at work.

Ultimately, precautions against poisonings or accidents caused by alcohol must be confined primarily to the responsibility of the individual. Few people are not aware of the dangers involved if they drink before driving – this is being recognised more and more by the courts as they quite rightly impose stiffer sentences.

Where medicines are concerned, the label should state clearly if it is dangerous for them to be taken with alcohol. If there is any doubt check with the prescribing doctor or chemist; never assume that it will be safe without making absolutely certain. Some non-prescribed medicines or treatments, such as sinusitis tablets, can cause drowsiness in conjunction with alcohol. This can lead to an increased likelihood of accidents whilst driving or operating machinery. For that matter, some of these substances can cause drowsiness without the presence of alcohol, so due care should be taken. Labels will advise of any such side effects.

Parental responsibility must also play a role where teenagers are concerned. Teenage parties and drinking sessions cause a great number of both poisonings and other alcohol-related accidents. Emphasising the dangers of drinking too much and dismissing the false belief that 'holding' large quantities of alcohol indicates masculinity may play some part in lessening the risks.

## Asbestos

Asbestos has been a much-publicised source of illness and disease, primarily because inhalation of the fibres can cause asbestosis, lung cancer and mesothelioma. Generally speaking, asbestos damages people who have an occupational exposure to its fibres, but all forms should be treated as having no safe dust or fibre exposure level.

**There are three main forms of the material, including white asbestos (chrysolite), brown asbestos (amosite) and blue asbestos (crocidolite). White asbestos is the most common of the three.**

Products that sometimes use or contain asbestos include oven gloves, oven door replacement seals, ironing board rests, simmering pads, car brake linings, insulation board, cement sheeting, fire-resistant lining materials and car underseals.

Any product suspected of containing asbestos should, if possible, be replaced. Avoid using any asbestos DIY products – drilling, sawing or sanding asbestos increases the airborne dust levels and thus increases the hazard.

The Asbestos Products (Safety) Regulations insist that DIY materials containing asbestos should be labelled with the letter 'A', and should be accompanied by relevant safety instructions. This advice includes working outdoors or in well-ventilated areas, and using hand or low-speed tools equipped, where necessary, with suitable dust extraction facilities. If high-speed tools are used they must always have extraction facilities.

**Users are also advised to dampen both the material and any dust with water and to dispose of dust safely in a sealed container. Even so, the best advice has always been: try to find a substitute!**

With domestic products that contain asbestos and cannot easily be replaced with a safer substitute, be particularly careful to watch for signs of wear and tear. In these products asbestos takes the form of a conditioned solid or spun cloth;

once the structure begins to decay, fibres are more likely to be released.

Asbestos panels or boards used in the construction of your home should also be checked for signs of decay. If the boards are old or damaged contact your local authority for advice about their removal. At the very least this should be done by a reputable builder aware of the risks posed by asbestos dust both to the home occupants and, perhaps more importantly, to his own workforce.

Panels that are not damaged and do not show signs of decay would probably be best left in place – removing them would actually be more likely to cause a dust hazard. Such panels can be sealed with paint to prevent any dust from escaping in the future; use emulsion paint for insulation board and an alkali-resistant primer for asbestos-cement products, which contain lime.

## Carbon monoxide

Carbon monoxide is an odourless, colourless gas produced as a byproduct of the incomplete combustion of many fuels, including domestic solid fuels, gas, burning materials in a house fire and petrol in a car engine.

Carbon monoxide is without question the chemical that causes the greatest number of fatal domestic poisonings every year. Indeed, between 1982 and 1983, 110 people were killed by carbon monoxide poisoning in this country, of whom the greatest number were the victims of accidents caused by gas or solid-fuel appliances. This figure does not include many fatalities caused by domestic fires in which carbon monoxide poisoning was the actual cause of death.

A significant reduction in the number of deaths caused by carbon monoxide coincided with the conversion from town or coal gas to natural gas. The reason for this was that coal gas had very high carbon monoxide concentrations (up to 30 per cent), whilst natural (or North-Sea) gas contains very little. In fact, whilst the number of domestic gas consumers rose from 12.4 million in 1967, when conversion from coal to natural gas started, to 14.9 million in 1981, the total number of people killed by unburnt gas, burnt gas or suicide by gas poisoning fell from 1,912 to 102. Nonetheless, about 80 of the fatalities involving carbon monoxide poisoning every year are caused by faulty or neglected gas appliances. One particularly important point is that most of these appliances were not installed by British Gas and had never been visited by their engineers.

**The chief hazards are those of blocked or faulty flues, inadequate ventilation, and gas appliances that have not been properly maintained or serviced.**

A combination of these factors can create potentially lethal situations. An appliance which is not burning the gas completely will produce high levels of carbon monoxide. Equally, an inadequate supply of oxygen to fuel the combustion will also lead to increased levels of the gas. Where ventilation is concerned, remember that burnt gas contains some carbon monoxide and that any gas appliance used without proper extraction flues or chimneys will be dangerous.

Ensure that all appliances are properly maintained. If you have any doubts about the installation of gas appliances, flues or your mains supply, contact British Gas for advice. Phone them as an emergency if you smell gas at all. Have flues and chimneys inspected occasionally to ensure they are clear.

Solid-fuel appliances such as coal central heating systems, cookers or stoves also present risks. These are usually caused by blocked chimneys or inadequate cleaning of the appliance.

One survey, by the Domestic Coal Consumers Council, revealed a frightening picture: more than half the families using a solid-fuel room heater failed to follow recommended safety precautions.

Almost half of the people who had appliances with a flue pipe thought the flue pipe did not need to be cleaned or checked and about 14 per cent said that their pipes were never checked. Even though chimneys ought to be swept at least once a year only 63 per cent of the respondents actually did this.

Cleaning the appliance is always important. This is done by removing the throat plate at the back and brushing out the accumulated dust and soot. Failure to do this prevents fumes from escaping and forces them to seep back into the home.

Other appliances can emit carbon monoxide, including

flued oil-burning appliances and portable gas or paraffin heaters if they are not well-maintained and used in well-ventilated areas.

**Balanced flue equipment, in which air is taken from the outside, avoids many of these hazards for gas appliances. Note that it is illegal to fit anything other than balanced flue water heaters in bathrooms.**

A number of accidents occur involving car exhaust fumes. Common circumstances where this risk arises include leaving the car engine running whilst in a closed garage. Always remember that car exhaust fumes contain a high level of carbon monoxide and that proper ventilation is crucial.

Be extremely cautious with all appliances that might produce carbon monoxide. Think carefully before purchasing second-hand equipment, and have it professionally serviced before use. Remember that the Gas Safety (Installation and Use) Regulations 1984 make the installation of a faulty gas appliance illegal. Watch out for signs that appliances are producing fumes within the home. Tell-tale indicators include discolouration and staining of both the appliance casing and the adjacent wall or fireplace.

## Cavity wall insulation

Doubts have been expressed in the United States about the safety of urea-formaldehyde foam (UF foam) for insulating cavity walls of buildings. These arise because the foam, which is injected through the outer wall and hardens after a time, gives off considerable quantities of formaldehyde vapours if the conditions (such as temperature) of preparation and curing are not carefully controlled.

The United States studies suggest that formaldehyde vapours may be responsible for a range of cancers, including nasal cancers. The official view in this country is that formaldehyde vapours of the concentrations encountered from cavity wall insulation do not cause nasal cancer, but that their link with other forms of cancer is still open to question. However, it is worth remembering that this country is notoriously slow in taking up health measures established as necessary abroad, with asbestos and its dangers presenting a good example. Until proven otherwise, UF foam should be treated as a potentially dangerous form of house insulation and its use avoided if possible.

At one stage, only firms registered under the British Standards Institution's Surveillance Scheme were allowed to inject UF foam as a cavity insulation. Part of this scheme ensured compliance with BS 5617 and BS 5618, two relevant standards. However, the controls formulated under the Building Regulations have now been relaxed with the effect that UF foam can only be used in cavity walls with an inner leaf of bricks and blocks but almost anybody can put it there. Safety measures are confined to taking all reasonable precautions to ensure that formaldehyde vapours do not permeate the building. The new controls are 'deemed to be satisfied' if the foam is injected in compliance with BS 5617 and BS 5618.

If you do decide to have UF foam cavity wall insulation, ensure that the firm that does this agrees to do it in accordance with BS 5617 and BS 5618. All firms registered with the BSI Registered Firms Scheme or members of the National Cavity Insulation Association can be relied upon to do this.

## Cosmetics

Cosmetics are not likely to cause poisonings. Lead is outlawed in cosmetics by the Cosmetic Products Regulations 1978. The only exception to this rule is the 'surma' eye make-up used by some Asian women. Surmas containing lead are sometimes brought into the country, something that has prompted a government campaign.

The Cosmetic Products Regulations are extremely precise in their definition of substances prohibited in cosmetics and in their definition of substances which can only be used in limited quantities. The regulations also prohibit the use of substances likely to cause harm from skin contact as well as those that would present a risk of poisoning by ingestion.

For the record, one report (by the Consumer Safety Unit of the Department of Trade and Industry) highlighted the following products as having been involved in accidents involving young children: hair treatments, soap, toothpastes, hair removers, make-up, shaving creams, bath oils and cubes, talcum powder, nail varnish (and remover), perfume and deodorants.

## Lead

Lead has been recognised as a poison for hundreds of years and steps have been taken to eliminate the kind of high exposure where it can prove fatal. Where exposure does still cause concern, however, is the general level of lead in people's blood streams, which in some reports has been estimated to be about a quarter of the level at which recognisable lead poisoning sometimes occurs.

In particular, researchers have been concerned by the manner in which low concentrations of lead can impair the intelligence and behaviour of small children. The main culprit is the lead contained in petrol and emitted in car exhaust fumes. The government has already announced plans to phase out the lead in petrol, something demanded of them by an EEC directive.

The use of lead in paint will be examined in the section on DIY Safety: Painting and Decorating.

Lead carried in water is an ingestion hazard, both in drinks and by the absorption by food of the lead during cooking. Old lead piping in houses can sometimes increase the lead level of water in soft water areas, but this is less likely to be a problem in hard water areas. Your local water authority will let you know if this is a hazard in your district. If it is, they can check the lead content of your water supply although they may ask you to pay a small charge for the service. Replacing lead pipes may, depending upon the circumstances, qualify for a home-improvements grant.

Hot water will increase the likelihood of lead piping dissolving, so water from the hot tap should not be used for drinking in a system where lead piping still exists, even if it has been boiled first. If a water softener is installed in your system you must check whether your plumbing includes lead pipes. If it does, a separate tap for drinking water must be fitted. Softened water that has passed through lead pipes must always be treated as a possible lead hazard and must never be drunk.

# SLIPS, TRIPS AND FALLS

It surprises some people to learn that most accidents in the home are caused by people simply falling over and hurting themselves. According to the 1984 HASS report, slipping, tripping and falling caused 62.8 per cent of all the accidents that resulted in in-patient treatment at hospital. The greatest proportion of these were caused by falling on the same level (i.e. tripping or slipping), closely followed by falling from stairs (12.6 per cent) and falling between two levels (12.2 per cent). The prominence of falling is equally apparent when the number of fatal accidents is examined. Across the country in 1983, falls of one sort or another killed 2,793 people, or 60.9 per cent of the total number of people killed in domestic accidents.

One of the main observations to be made from a comparison of the two sets of figures is that falling between two levels and slipping and tripping on the same level figure no less prominently as causes of fatalities than they do as causes of minor accidents. This huge source of suffering and injury in the home far exceeds sports like skiing, hang-gliding or rock climbing in its toll, yet most houses are beset with potential falling, tripping or slipping risks. Stairs are littered with toys, carpets and rugs are loose, electric cables are left draped over the floor and rickety step ladders or untied ladders are used with abandon. Part of the reason for this, of course, is that walking about the house is not as dangerous for young or middle-aged people as rock climbing or hang-gliding! But for the very young or the elderly it can be, comparatively speaking, as dangerous, and it is the very young and the elderly who figure prominently in the accident statistics. In fact, the under-14s and over-65s accounted between them for over 60 per cent of all the non-fatal falls in the 1984 HASS report.

## Staircases

Staircases are one of the most obvious hazards. Ensure that lighting is adequate and is used! It is no good having excellent lighting throughout if it is not used in the evening or at night. The tops and the bottoms of staircases should have a child gate if small children are in the house. Child barriers of this sort (which can also be fitted across doorways) should conform to BS 4125.

Carpets must be well fitted, with horizontal carpet rods securely in place if they are used. Check that carpets are not worn or frayed. It has been suggested that laying carpets with the pile sloping upwards helps to prevent falls.

Handrails are essential for all types of stair, preferably on both sides. Make sure that the gap between the individual uprights is not so great that children can slip through.

Outdoor or uncarpeted stairs can be treated with a white, yellow or reflective strip along the upper edge of each stair, something that is particularly useful for poorly lit stairwells. Typical cases where this might be needed include cellar stairs or back door steps.

## Stair-lifts

Disabled or elderly people may find it necessary to have a powered stair-lift fitted. This should conform to BS 5776 which gives minimum safety rules for the design, construction, installation, operation and maintenance of all power-driven stair-lifts. Your local social services will be able to advise if you are eligible for any financial help.

## Carpets, rugs and mats

Joins between different types of floor covering, such as between linoleum and carpet, should always be sealed with an aluminium (or similar) strip. This prevents either surface from lifting and causing someone to trip. Rugs, mats or door mats should be firmly fixed if they are on a slippery surface. Rugs are quite secure on carpets, but they are potentially lethal on polyurethaned floorboarding.

Spills of liquids should be mopped up immediately after they occur. This is of particular importance in the bathroom or kitchen. In the kitchen be careful to clean up spills of fat with detergent. Do not cover with newspaper as a temporary measure – the paper could slip if anyone steps on it.

## Other causes of slips and falls

Also remember that the injuries caused by trips and falls can be compounded by other factors. For instance, never walk about carrying a knife – sit down at a work surface or table to use it. Equally, you should switch off certain types of electrical appliances before moving them. Hair driers, irons, electric drills and similar appliances are designed to function while moving but with equipment like portable televisions, the description 'portable' only means that they can be carried from one place to another, not that they should be moved while switched on.

**When cooking, make sure that pan handles do not stick out. Remember they will usually be at an ideal height for someone to fall against or for toddlers to grab hold of.**

Children should never be left unattended on beds, sofas, chairs or any other surfaces they could fall off. Always use safety harnesses (on highchairs, pushchairs and so on) properly and check that equipment for children is in a good state of repair.

Keep flexes short and well out of the way. Trailing flexes cause a great number of accidents every year.

Snow and ice can cause slips and falls especially among elderly people. In comparatively moderate winters, digging up pathways and steps, and covering them with salt should keep them clear. Occasionally, however, winters in this country are cold enough to freeze salted surfaces. Grit has the advantage that it provides a rough surface thereby enhancing the grip of people walking on it.

Bathrooms used by elderly or disabled people should be fitted with handrails on both sides of the bath. Various types of non-slip mat are available for the bottom of showers and baths; these are usually rubber with suction pads underneath and should always be used for baby baths.

## *Ladders*

Ladders and stepladders can be dangerous. The latter must be fully extended and be on a firm base. The former should be at an angle of between 70° and 75° to the ground, and should be tied to something at the top – either to an external fixture or, through a window, to something firmly anchored inside. It is a good idea to put heavy objects around the base of the ladder to stop it slipping. Always try to have someone standing at the foot of the ladder while you are working. Do not tie yourself to the top of the ladder – if the ladder does fall, your trajectory to the ground could be increased by virtue of the fact that you are tied to its top! It is far safer to make sure you don't

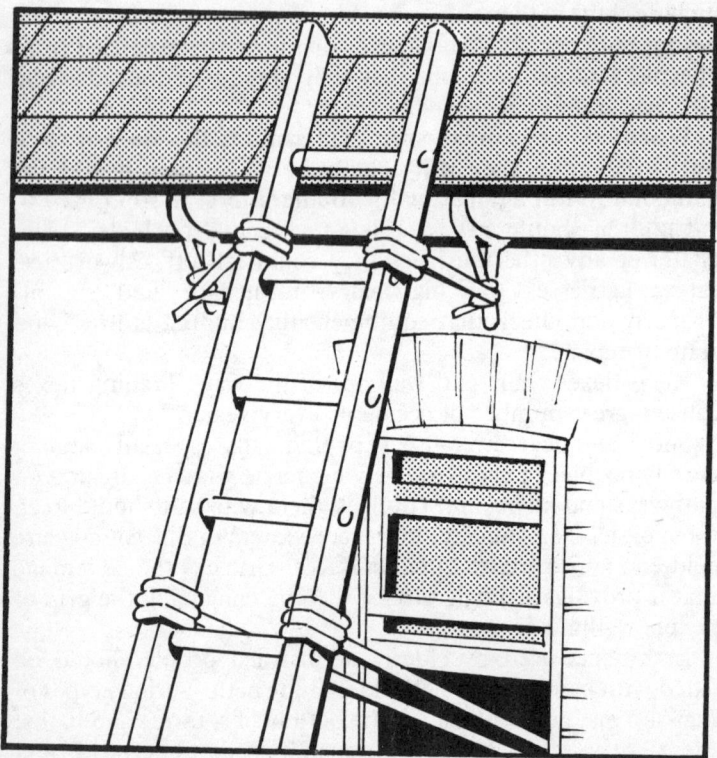

Ladders should always be tied securely

overstretch during your work and that you always try to keep one hand on the ladder.

**Wooden ladders should be kept in good condition and inspected regularly. Metal ladders stay in better condition and are lighter, but these are more prone to slipping and 'whipping', and must be kept away from any overhead power cables.**

One extra risk from slipping or falling is that of smashing interior glass panels, screens or doors. Methods of limiting these risks include highlighting the glass (see p.8), replacing it with wood, or replacing it with toughened glass.

## Glass

Most household glass is cheap, 'annealed' or sheet glass. This shatters easily and breaks into large, sharp splinters and portions. With glass in doors, door surrounds, interior screens and panels, replacing sheet glass with toughened or 'tempered' glass might be a good idea. Tempered glass is essentially ordinary glass that has been tempered with heat to soften its brittleness. Whilst it is more expensive than ordinary glass, it will only break with a really hard blow and even then will shatter into thousands of minute and comparatively harmless fragments.

Other forms of safety glass include laminated glass (see p.109), which should only be used with care, and plastics.

# GARDENING

The Department of Trade and Industry estimates that there are more than 100,000 accidents every year in gardens in the United Kingdom. These accidents are most frequently caused by power tools such as lawnmowers and hedgetrimmers. This is because of the combination of their high-speed cutting action and their electrical supply, both of which are capable of causing serious injury. On average there are seven or eight people fatally electrocuted in accidents involving lawnmowers every year.

Even so, wheelbarrows, forks, spades and other garden tools cause nearly as many accidents, emphasising that it would be dangerous to treat the garden as a place of recreation presenting only one form of risk. Even sunbeds and deckchairs cause a number of accidents! Other possible causes of accidents include fishponds, chemicals, bonfires, barbecues and a host of additional activities common in the garden.

Most of these accidents are the result of thoughtlessness and can be avoided with a little sensible planning, a few simple precautions and a little extra work.

## Electrical equipment

There is no real excuse for the number of accidents involving electrical garden equipment every year. All power tools are designed to high standards for simple and safe use.

### Mowers and hedgetrimmers

Metal bladed hover and rotary mowers, and hedgetrimmers

are the most frequent causes of accidents. By contrast, cylinder mowers account for a comparatively small proportion. Only buy those tools that have a BEAB or Kitemark – this will show that they have been properly tested and approved in accordance with the relevant British Standards.

## Cables and flexes

Extension leads for appliances that have three core cables must always be three core themselves. With the 'connector' type of extension cable, always ensure that the 'female' portion is fixed to the live end and the 'male' portion to the appliance end. This prevents any live parts being easily accessible. Keep cables well away from cutting edges and machinery during operation. The best way to do this is probably to run the cable over your shoulder and hold a loop in your hand.

Under no circumstances tamper with any electrical equipment whilst it is connected to the power source. Always unplug the appliance (and/or extension cable) first.

You are strongly advised to protect garden equipment with an RCCB (see p.23), either in a plug, an adaptor or fitted within the mains.

Coiled, ready-made cables must always be fully unwound before use to prevent the cables overheating inside their casing. This could lead to electrical faults or fires.

Never use electrical garden tools in the rain. Always connect the extension lead to the appliance cable before plugging the extension into the mains.

**Ensure that extension leads have a sufficient current capacity for the power rating of the tool. The wattage of the tool will be marked on its casing.**

Do not use extension cables as permanent fittings to power, for instance, the lighting or heating in a potting shed or greenhouse. Only use extension leads with rubber connectors outdoors. These are designed to shield against dampness.

Outdoor power sockets for electrical equipment can be used, but must be the waterproofed and metal type specially designed for that purpose. These have a screw-on cap to protect the terminals when they are not in use. Equipment powered by these must be protected by an RCCB.

Any electrical work of this sort should be done by a qualified electrician. Ensure that they are on the roll of the National Inspection Council for Electrical Installation Contracting (NICEIC). A list of such contractors in your area should be obtainable from your local electricity board.

The safest form of lawnmower is the hand mower. If you need a power mower, however, choose the cylinder type. Official statistics show that these, whether petrol or electric, are less likely to be involved in an accident.

## Using tools

One of the main dangers of the hover and rotary mowers is that people tend to swing them from side to side like a vacuum cleaner, thus increasing the chance of catching the cable or their foot. Never do this. Instead, walk forward pushing the mower in a straight line. Pick up any twigs, stones or other obstructions; these may impair the efficiency of the cutter or cause an accident if they come into contact with the blades.

**Always wear sturdy boots with rubber soles. These will both protect your feet in the event of an accident and offer some protection against electric shock.**

When cutting grass slopes or banks, mow across the slope with cylinder or rotary mowers. With hover mowers, stand on the level ground at the top and mow downwards. Be careful not to overstretch or slip. Make sure that electric mowers have safety lock switches to prevent accidental starting, and keep children and pets well away from the working area. It is now possible to buy rotary and vacuum mowers fitted with plastic safety blades. These can cut all types of grass throughout the mowing season. Equally, metal bladed machines can sometimes have optional plastic blade conversion kits but these have some drawbacks, for example, they can only be used for certain conditions of grass.

Hedgetrimmers should always be kept clear of the flex; drape this over one shoulder. Always allow enough free flex to permit full mobility.

**Keep both hands on the trimmer handles and never overstretch. If using a stepladder, make sure it is fully extended and standing on firm, level ground. If this is not**

possible, get somebody to stand on the bottom for you.

Try to buy a trimmer with hand guards. Never be tempted to remove clippings from the hedge with one hand whilst the trimmer is still running.

# Other hazards

## Handtools

Always wear strong leather boots when using handtools (in this context, handtools include forks, spades, hoes and so on – accidents with forks are far from unknown). Avoid wearing flimsy or open-toed footwear on dug soil even if not using a tool – broken glass or metal can cause unpleasant and dirty cuts. With this risk in mind, ensure that tetanus injections are kept up to date. In a typical year, up to 20 people might die from tetanus in this country. If you do cut yourself deeply, seek medical assistance.

## Glass

If you build cold frames or other constructions from glass, be careful to protect any exposed edges with plastic shielding or tape. Avoid using old, broken panes of glass with jagged or sharp edges. Canvas gloves with suede palms are always advisable for garden work.

## Storing tools

Do not leave tools lying around where they could be stepped on or tripped over. Keep tools stored safely, preferably hanging up out of the reach of children. Keep cutting tools such as secateurs sharp and well maintained. Chemicals used in the garden must be treated with the same caution as those in the home or DIY workshop.

## Fishponds

Do not forget that small children can drown in only three

inches of water. Keep all fishponds and water butts fenced off and strictly out of bounds. Paddling pools should be used under strict supervision only.

## Bonfires

Whether for bonfire night, for barbecues or simply to get rid of garden rubbish, bonfires should always be treated with care. Never start bonfires with petrol. Use newspaper, firelighters and dry twigs to get them burning. Never try to resuscitate a flagging fire by throwing petrol, paraffin or oil on to it. Remember that some materials give off poisonous fumes as they burn, or even explode. Do not burn aerosols, plastics or rubber. Concrete will also explode if subjected to high temperatures so build the bonfire on an earth base.

Keep bonfires small and under control. Have buckets of water or a connected (but not running!) hosepipe at the ready. Do not build 'top heavy' fires that could topple over and do not build bonfires near hedges, trees or buildings. Hawthorn and holly will burn fiercely even when they are green.

When the fire has finished, ensure it is completely out before leaving it; rake out the ashes and douse them with lots of water to make sure.

Keep flammable chemicals well away from fires and barbecues. With barbecues, use only long-handled cooking instruments and make sure that food is well cooked before serving – food often takes longer to cook on a barbecue. Use only the recommended fuel and supervise children closely. When the barbecue is finished, douse with water.

## Furniture

Garden furniture causes a surprising number of accidents, usually resulting in trapped (or even broken) fingers. Always check that joints and legs are in good condition and are firmly positioned on the ground. Check that seats and canvas covers are in good condition.

## Window boxes

Window boxes or flower pots on ledges must be well back from the edge. Window boxes on upper windows should be fixed securely.

## Paving

Paved areas or pathways can become slippery when wet. Try to construct them from non-slip materials. Keep all areas like this clear of dead leaves, which become especially slippery during periods of damp weather.

## Lifting and carrying

Some gardening work involves an element of demanding physical labour. Be particularly careful to follow the correct procedures for lifting and carrying heavy weights (see p.135). Do not try to take on tasks unless you are sure they are within your physical capabilities.

## Pruning trees

Do not attempt to cut down or prune large trees unless you are absolutely confident in your technical expertise. Climbing more than ten feet from the ground without specialist (and expensive) harnesses and safety lines can be dangerous and should be avoided.

**Branches that appear healthy will often be rotten inside; assessing whether or not a branch is safe to stand on is in itself a specialist task, as is calculating which way a branch or trunk will fall once it has been cut.**

Quite apart from your own safety (and that of any hapless passers-by), the welfare of the tree can be damaged by amateurish pruning! Hiring a professional company or tree surgeon could well prove the best and safest solution for everybody concerned.

# CHILD SAFETY

By and large, the rules for protecting children are the same as those for adults, except that they have to be imposed! Throughout every section of this book, we have tried to explore the special provisions required for children with each risk that comes along. There are, however, a number of risks encountered only by children that require particular mention.

## Toys

Supervising children while they are playing with their toys and carefully matching toys with children of the correct age are sensible precautions that can be completely negated if the toy itself does not come up to an acceptable standard of safety and manufacture. Most of the dangerous toys that compose the 'black museums' of trading standards officers up and down the country are cheap, imported imitations of traditional patterns. As a general rule, only buy toys made in this country.

**It is very important that you should be your own 'toy inspector' when buying toys. Do not be afraid to check toys thoroughly yourself. If this means asking the shopkeeper to open the box or packaging – do so!**

Only buy toys where the maker's name is on the toy or the container. If possible, buy toys that conform to BS 3443 or BS 5665. Try to buy toys that are non-flammable. In general, natural materials are safer than synthetic materials, but if in doubt, don't buy it! Check that toys are securely held together, and not by nails or wire. Make sure that toys have no jagged edges and that any clockwork mechanisms are securely enclosed. Toys that use powerful springs should be avoided altogether. Children give toys a hard time and will insist on putting things in their mouth. Make sure that eyes, noses and other small bits are securely fixed on. Don't be afraid to give them a good tug in the shop.

Electric toys should have a voltage of 20 volts or less. A transformer should be used if the current is to be supplied from the mains.

Avoid gimmicky novelties such as expanding toys, scented erasers, 'magic' candles that reignite, and such like. Even though many of these have been banned they still resurface from time to time. If you do come across suspect toys in the shops, complain to your trading standards office. Your town hall will put you in touch.

# Pushchairs, car seats and baby walkers

Pushchairs should conform to BS 4792. Generally, all those produced by major manufacturers meet a high standard of safety. Check that there are no folding joints or mechanisms that could trap a child's fingers. Be careful with the light-weight models. These often do not have a shopping tray and can easily topple over backwards if a heavy bag of shopping is slung over their handles.

Baby walkers should conform to the standards of BS 4648. Babies in cars should always be protected by a safety seat. There are two main types available for infants: rearward facing seats and carrycot restraints. While carrycot restraints are cheaper, the straps can break easily and they do not restrain the movement of the child. The rearward facing restraints are altogether better. These should conform to BS AU 202 or ECE (European Standard) 44. The traditional safety seats are meant for children old enough to sit up. These should conform to BS 3254 or ECE 44.

**Under no circumstances allow a child to sit unrestrained on somebody's lap. Remember that carrying an unrestrained baby in the front seat is illegal.**

## *Other points to remember*

Children have to be properly supervised when near to water. Everybody should wear a lifejacket when boating or yachting; children must. Teach children to swim at the earliest possible age. Young boys often want to go fishing – make sure it is on a safe, well-attended stretch of water and that there is proper adult supervision. If this means that mum or dad have to learn to fish as well – grin and bear it!

Small children old enough to crawl or toddle can be a nightmare. Most children's shops supply socket guards, fireguards and other sensible provisions.

Encourage children to develop safety consciousness. Organisations such as RoSPA (the Royal Society for the Prevention of Accidents) in Birmingham have a number of excellent schemes and clubs for children – contact them for further information.

# SECURITY

At one time many safety experts might have argued that protecting property and possessions did not fall within the scope of 'safety' as such and consequently the subject might have been considered out of place in a book such as this. However, the ever-increasing wave of break-ins and violent assaults renders this view obsolete; the fact is that people do run the risk of being burgled, and it is possible that the person who breaks in will be violent. This is sufficient to justify considering security as part of safety.

Before looking at individual aspects of risk and possible remedies, remember that the services of two people can be called upon to help you. The first of these is your Crime Prevention Officer (CPO). Every police station has a CPO who will be willing to give you, in complete confidence, a free security survey. CPOs are sensitive to all the problems facing people, including finance, and will suggest the most reasonable and cost effective way of keeping your home secure.

The second person who may be of use is your Fire Prevention Officer (FPO). It is fairly easy to fit elaborate locks to all possible entrances into your home, effectively preventing uninvited access, but in doing so there is the danger that you might also effectively prevent yourself from escaping from a fire, or inadvertently hinder the fire brigade from gaining access if you are trapped inside. If you suspect that your security system might cause these problems contact your FPO for advice.

Almost everybody is allowed to improve the security of their home. The Housing Act 1980 gives council tenants the right to carry out a range of improvements to their home, including replacing internal or external doors and fitting or replacing locks and bolts. Council tenants do not need the permission of the council to do this. Private tenants should obtain the permission of their landlords before doing any improvement work of this sort. Even so, the landlord cannot unreasonably withhold permission.

## Mortice locks

The most common secure lock is the mortice. This is designed to fit into a mortice (or chiselled slot) cut into the edge of the door. One of its great strengths is that it is not screwed to the surface – to force the door, an intruder would also have to force the timber. However, this can be a weakness if the door is rotten or in a bad state of repair; replacing the door might be as important as replacing the lock! Many mortice locks also have a spring bolt (similar to that of a latch) controlled by the door handle. These are known as sash locks.

## Latches

Various types of the popular latch lock exist. Spring latches have a shaped bolt that can be pushed back into the lock case. These are not secure and can be opened with a strip of plastic quite easily. Dead latches have a bolt that is rigidly extended once locked and are far preferable. Even so, both types are surface mounted.

Dead latches can be double-locking. This means that an extra, opposite turn of the key from the outside when locking the door deadlocks both the bolt and the handle. This would prevent a would-be intruder from breaking a glass panel in the door (if there is one) and putting a hand inside to turn the handle of the lock. Some dead latches also have an auxiliary bolt that automatically deadlocks the latch bolt when the door is closed. When you turn the key in the lock, it functions by moving the 'lever'. The lever has a variety of cuts in its underside to provide a combination that is in principle unique to one key. In fact, there are a comparatively small number of permutations per lever. Consequently, the greater the number of levers inside the lock, the harder it will be for someone to duplicate the key.

## Builders' locks

Some back doors still have two-lever locks (also known as builders' original locks). These are not reliable, as a burgler only needs a set of 12 keys to be sure of finding one that will fit.

All external locks should be five lever. Changing a two-lever mortice lock for one with five levers should not be difficult. Since the late 1950s the major British lock manufacturers have made their mortice locks to the same specifications. Providing that your two-lever lock was fitted either during or after this period, replacing it will simply be a matter of taking the old lock out and putting the new one in – the mortice size, key hole and screw holes should all be the right size and in the right place.

## Chains and viewers

Front doors can also be fitted with door chains and door viewers, both of which are comparatively cheap, efficient and easy to put in place.

## Hinge locks and mortice bolts

If external doors have hinges on the outside, fit hinge bolts. These are simply bolts on the hinge edge of the door that swing into holes in the door post as the door closes. If somebody unscrews the hinges, the door will still be firmly and securely held in place.

Outside doors (or 'final exit' doors) should be secured with concealed mortice bolts as well as their other locks. These are fitted in a similar way to mortice locks and are operated by a fluted key. Two bolts should be fitted – one at the top and one at the bottom of the door.

## Windows

Windows are a potential security risk because a burglar need only break the glass to gain entry with most traditional fittings and locks. Extra effort, therefore, must be made to deter any intruder seeking easy entry. Sash windows can be opened surprisingly easily by levering the lower (inside) frame upwards with screwdrivers or with a jemmy forced under it at the sill. Occasionally, a knife forced between the frames will be enough to turn the catch.

Locks are available for all types of window, including casement, sash and fanlight windows. Windows operated by a perforated arm can also be fitted with a lock incorporating the vertical bolt used as a stay.

**Ensure that locks conform to BS 3621, which requires a high level of security performance. Many manufacturers belong to the Kitemark scheme, giving even further guarantees.**

## Burglaries

The majority of break-ins occur through windows (61 per cent), and of these 48 per cent are through windows at the back of the building. The back door lets in 16 per cent of all burglars, but the front door, perhaps a little surprisingly, is even more popular, accounting for 20 per cent of recorded cases. Side doors are not popular at all (2 per cent), something shared by side windows (6 per cent).

Some authorities have calculated that there is a burglary every minute of the day and night and that everybody has a one-in-three chance of being burgled at least once during their lifetime. These conclusions emphasise the importance of checking the high risk areas of your house and of securing them thoroughly.

Be careful of new doors that look nice! Wooden panels in doors are often easier and quieter to break through than panes of glass, and small panes of glass can sometimes be completely removed by a determined thief.

Surface mounted draw bolts are easy game for the villain, who only has to make a hole, either in an adjacent window or through the wood, before it is possible to pull the bolt and gain access.

Modern patio doors are safer than they used to be, but these may still need a multi-point locking system or cylinder lock. Ask your CPO for advice.

Beware of laminated glass. This, in effect, is a layer of transparent plastic sandwiched between two layers of glass. The plastic, polyvinyl butyral, prevents the glass from being smashed. Whilst the glass will splinter and crack, it stays in one piece. This presents obvious dangers for anyone needing to escape during a fire. Laminated glass should only be used for domestic glazing after professional advice has been sought.

## Burglar alarms

Burglar alarms do deter people from attempting to break in where they are prominently displayed on the outside of a building. They are not very expensive and DIY kits are available. The only part that the DIY enthusiast might find troublesome would be the wiring. The system can be set to trigger off an alarm for a period of time in the hope that a neighbour or passer-by will hear it, or to inform a monitoring station who then call the police. Do not forget that alarms do not prevent people from breaking in, but merely deter them. Your local police station should be able to give you a list of installers in your area and your CPO will advise on the type of system most suited to your needs and resources.

## Door entry systems

When a number of flats or dwellings share a common front door, an entry-phone system can be installed. Remember, however, that these are only as safe and secure as the individual residents choose to make them. If somebody does let a stranger in, the separate flats will have to rely upon the security of their own front doors, something that should not be neglected. Some systems now have closed circuit television as an additional safeguard.

## Safety on the street

Many attacks and assaults occur while people, mainly women, are outside the home. Self-defence classes may offer some help in a difficult situation but it is obviously more desirable to avoid the situation in the first place. Avoid taking short cuts through poorly lit areas or alleyways, and never accept lifts from strangers or hitch hike. Buy a personal alarm, which is usually in the form of a small aerosol of compressed gas that emits a loud shrieking noise when activated. Keep the alarm in an accessible place – even walk with it in your hand, perhaps in your pocket, if you feel the situation demands it.

**Security in any situation like this is a matter of thinking safely.**

Walking towards the traffic, for instance, makes it a little more difficult for somebody in a car to pull up beside you.

Inside the house, never let strangers on the phone know if you are alone, especially if you are a woman. Equally, single women should use their surname and initials only (with no title) on door plates or in the phone book.

## Going on holiday

The welfare of your home while you are on holiday is only the business of a book on safety in so much as fires and other accidents can occur in an empty house if sensible precautions are not taken. Be careful to turn off the gas, water and electricity. Provisions for electrical equipment that must be left on while you are away have already been discussed (see p.70).

Lock all ladders, tools and other DIY equipment away as securely as you lock your doors and windows. Cancel all regular deliveries such as milk or newspapers. Mowing lawns and trimming hedges might be a good idea if you are going to be away for a time.

Let the police know you will be away and for how long. Equally, leave the key with a friend or neighbour.

Electrical time switches (similar to those used for central heating systems) can be bought quite cheaply. These basically consist of a clock dial on an adaptor with a socket. Whilst you are away they can be used to switch a light on in one of your front rooms and turn it off in the morning. Curtains and blinds should be left open.

# SAFETY ON THE ROADS

Safe driving is not something that strictly speaking falls within the scope of this book; the Highway Code is, in effect, a legal document since it explains the rules of driving that must, by law, be followed.

Other groups of road users, however, do deserve special mention. Prime amongst these are pedestrians and cyclists, perhaps because both groups sometimes fail to take themselves seriously as road users, even though both are covered by the Highway Code.

The rules of safety for pedestrians: wearing light-coloured clothing in the evening, the Green Cross Code for crossing roads, walking into rather than with the traffic and so on, have been more than adequately drummed into the heads of most people at school. They are formulated for sensible reasons and should be followed at all times. Parents should teach their children to regard the roads with caution from the earliest possible age.

Safe cycling is examined in some depth at the end of the section. Car drivers should already have a copy of the Highway Code – if not, get one! The safety of children in cars is examined in the section on Child safety, and personal safety while maintaining cars is covered in the section on DIY safety.

## Alcohol and the road user

The dangers of alcohol poisoning have been mentioned elsewhere, but the massive accident toll caused by the combination of drinking and driving cannot pass unmentioned. The facts speak for themselves. According to the

Transport and Road Research Laboratory, one tenth of all injuries in car accidents occur from driving with excess alcohol in the blood. One third of all drivers and motorcycle riders killed have alcohol levels above the legal limit.

**On Friday and Saturday nights between 10 p.m. and 4 a.m., two thirds of drivers and riders killed have alcohol levels above the legal limit. In total, more than one thousand people are killed every year as the result of drinking and driving. This is the equivalent of three Jumbo jets crashing!**

The reason for these accidents is that alcohol reduces muscular control, co-ordination, reactions, vision and judgement. All these make accidents more likely. Alcohol also affects judgement of one's own state – it can even make you genuinely believe you are driving and performing better than you are.

Legal limits are a little misleading. The legal limit for alcohol in the blood while driving is 80 mg per 100 ml, 107 mg per 100 ml for urine and 35 micrograms per 100 ml for breath. But the performance of young or inexperienced drivers will be seriously impaired well below this level, as will that of people who only drink occasionally.

It is impossible to calculate blood alcohol levels accurately from the quantity consumed, as factors such as body weight, whether the drinker has a full stomach and how rapidly they have been drinking must also be taken into account.

In general, drivers should avoid drinking on empty stomachs, should drink slowly, eat while drinking and stop drinking some time before driving. The quantity consumed should be confined to three units. One unit of alcohol is considered to be half a pint of beer or cider, a third of a pint of strong beer or cider, a glass of wine or sherry, or a single measure of whisky. Remember that measures of spirit are 20 per cent larger in Scotland than in England, and 50 per cent larger in Northern Ireland.

# Safe cycling

Cycling is becoming an extremely popular means of transport

and for understandable reasons. Leaving the car in the garage and pedalling to work is more than just cheap and healthy – it is also an ideal way to bypass the congestion of busy city roads. Cycling in the countryside and on touring holidays is also gaining in popularity.

The cyclist on the road, however, is vulnerable. There are two main reasons for this: bicycles are small (and thus difficult for motorists to see) and they offer no protection to the person riding them in the event of a crash. The proof of this is to be found in the accident statistics. An estimated 30,000 cyclists were killed or injured on Britain's roads in 1986. The biggest increase is amongst children in the 15 to 19 age group. In fact, children account for 35 per cent of all casualties. Males of all ages are more likely to have accidents than females – four times more likely to be precise.

A cyclist is at greatest risk of an accident in the city. Ninety per cent of all accidents occur in built-up areas. Eighty per cent of all accidents involving children occur on housing estates, minor roads and suburban streets. Adult accidents, however, are more likely to occur on major roads. The most dangerous places for cyclists are those near junctions and roundabouts where approximately 70 per cent of accidents happen. Whilst the blame for this may often lie with motorists who do not look properly before pulling out of or into junctions, the responsibility obviously lies with cyclists to anticipate the motorist's oversight.

Matters of particular concern include behaviour on the roads, visibility (including lighting) and proper maintenance of the machine.

## Motorists

There are things that drivers can do to minimise the risks they present to cyclists. The most important, not surprisingly, is to make a particular effort to look out for cyclists. An adult on a cycle, seen from the front, only occupies about a quarter of the width of a car. People who hit cyclists don't do it on purpose – but they often do it because they don't notice the bike approaching.

**Be careful when turning into side roads, especially to the**

**right. If you are waiting for an oncoming vehicle to pass before turning to the right avoid concentrating on the gap and the next vehicle behind it alone – make sure that the nearest vehicle is not concealing a cyclist or motorcycle from view.**

Motorists should also be careful when turning out of side streets, onto main roads or pulling out into roundabouts. Give cycles as much room as possible, especially if the rider is a child. Be prepared for erratic or unpredictable movement and remember that cyclists may not follow the Highway Code exactly on complex roads or roundabouts. Always make a special effort to watch out for cyclists at dusk, when the contrast between light and dark is at its minimum.

## Cyclists

Cyclists must act defensively. Always assume that motorists have not seen you and be prepared to brake suddenly when approaching junctions. Watch out for parked cars with people sitting in them – thoughtlessly opened doors can knock cyclists over, perhaps into the path of another vehicle.

Where motorists are waiting to pull out of, or into, side roads or junctions, always try to make eye contact directly with the driver. Do not forget that riding a bicycle does not exempt you from the Highway Code – cyclists are legally obliged to follow its guidelines like anyone else. When starting a journey, try to pull out from the left kerb and only do so when there is a clear space in the traffic. Do not cycle over kerbs – not only does this ruin wheels, it can also lead to cycles wobbling or skidding. When riding on the straight, look out for children, dogs or anything else that might move into the road and pose a danger.

**Avoid carrying heavy loads without proper panniers, saddlebags or carriers. Never hang bags of shopping over the handlebars, where they can destabilise steering, or at the rear, where they can catch in moving mechanisms.**

Never carry passengers unless (of course) the cycle is a tandem, or (in the case of children) has a proper child seat. Think carefully about the wisdom of the latter practice before embarking on it.

Keep a good, safe distance behind other vehicles, and give way to pedestrians at crossings – being on a cycle does not give you licence to slip through pelican or zebra crossings! Always look behind before any manoeuvre. Only change direction if the traffic is clear and always give a hand signal in plenty of time. If turning to the right across the stream of oncoming traffic, look behind before taking up position in the centre of the road. If there is not a clear space in your lane of the traffic, pull in to the left and wait for one. The same must be done when pulling out from a side road intending to turn right. Roundabouts can be a headache. Experienced adult cyclists who can keep up with the cars would probably be better, when turning right (or taking the third exit) to behave like a car themselves and move into the right hand (inner) lane. If you are not sure of yourself, however, keep to the left, or dismount and walk round!

**Many cyclists are now wearing personal stereos while they are riding their bikes. This is a foolish and potentially fatal practice. In many ways, hearing is as important as sight on a bike – wearing headphones is no less stupid than cycling blindfolded.**

Unlike with motorcyclists, there is no legal requirement for cyclists to wear helmets. There is, however, a lot to be said in favour of wearing one of the many safety helmets available from all good dealers. These are mostly reasonably cheap, and those designed for racing cyclists are neither cumbersome to wear nor ungainly in appearance.

Be careful if toe clips are fitted to the pedals. These can take some getting used to, especially on the busy roads of a city where feet are frequently taken out of the pedals. Watch for long, trailing loops of shoe lace – these can catch round pedal cranks and jam the mechanism, to say nothing of trapping a foot on the pedal.

Avoid cycling in winter weather. Bicycle tyres simply do not grip on snow and ice and the dangers of cycling in traffic on icy roads are not worth the risk.

## Staying visible

Lamps can be powered either by batteries or by a dynamo, and should be fitted to the front of the bike, where they must be clearly visible and white, and to the rear, where they must be clearly visible and red. Front lights should conform to BS AU 155 or BS 6102, and rear lights to BS 3648 or BS 6102.

Front lamps should be mounted so that they point straight forward and slightly down, while rear lamps must point straight behind and must not be allowed to point up or down, left or right. Both the front and the rear lights should be fitted on the right hand side of the bike or, with some models, at the centre. Never put lights on the left hand side of the bike where they may be hidden from sight. Be careful that lights, particularly those at the rear, do not become obscured by panniers or any other fixture. Always carry spare batteries and bulbs. Make sure that replacement bulbs have the same power rating as those in the lamps.

By law, bikes must also have a rear reflector when they are ridden at night. The legal definition of the period when both reflectors and lamps must be used is lighting-up time (half an hour after sunset until half an hour before sunrise). For all practical purposes the period when the street lights are on is a good guide.

Small, round reflectors satisfy the law, but bigger, more effective models are available. Reflectors should be fitted to either the centre or to the right of the bike, and should be neither too high nor too low. Rear reflectors should be red; those at the front, where they are used, should be white. Rear reflectors should conform to either BS 6102, BS AU 40L or be marked E. Bicycles manufactured after October 1, 1985 should be fitted with amber pedal reflectors. Keep all reflectors and lamps clean.

Reflective strips, jackets, putties and other items of clothing are available. These are surprisingly effective, and enhance the individual's visibility considerably.

## Maintenance

Bikes must be kept well maintained at all times. Very little is needed to do this; a good manual and a basic tool kit will do for most work.

Check that your frame is not damaged. In particular, look for damaged forks – these may bend or collapse in the event of a crash. Bearings (wheels, bottom bracket, headset and pedals) should be neither too tight nor too loose and must not be damaged. Bearings that constantly need adjusting probably need replacing too!

Brakes and gears must have good, tight cables. Look for signs of fraying or rust, and lubricate all exposed lengths. Brakes must be properly fixed and set. Centre pull brakes need the least maintenance and are much cheaper than they used to be. Make sure that brake blocks are not worn and that the closed end of the shoe is facing forwards. Keep tyres well inflated and replace them if they show signs of damage or wear. Other accessories to check include the saddle, chain, pedals, gear mechanisms, mud guards and lamps. Many of the guides available from bike shops give more detailed, step-by-step instructions.

# DIY SAFETY

At one time or another most of the households in Britain become host to some of the activities known collectively as 'Do It Yourself '.

The degree of enthusiasm for this varies from one individual to another; at one end of the spectrum are the people who do no more than hang a picture or replace a pane of glass; at the other end are those people who construct and equip elaborate workshops that approximate in some cases to the kind of working environment found in light industry.

The 1984 HASS report explored the number of DIY accidents in some depth. No fewer than 73 different DIY tools, products or substances featured in the accidents. The most frequently-mentioned items included non-domestic knives (1,081 accidents), pieces of wood (1,280) and screws and tacks (1,719).

DIY can prove fatal as well as fruitful. In 1983, DIY tools and equipment alone were involved in 103 of the deaths recorded. Whilst this is not an especially large proportion of the total (4,592), it does remain one of the most significant categories of fatal accident (eighth in a list of forty-four).

Just as DIY workshops may sometimes resemble those of light industry, so do the dangers and the hazards which they present. The information in this section is meant to supplement material elsewhere in this book. Obviously, the rules of electrical safety are basically the same in the home as they are in the DIY workshop; the special functions and activities of the workshop, however, mean that the rules may need enlargement and redefinition in places.

# DIY and the law

We mentioned in the Introduction that the Health and Safety at Work Act does not apply to the home but only to your place of work. This is largely true of your workshop as well; because you do not earn a living from your DIY activities they do not fall under the auspices of the Act. In those few cases where people do earn a living from DIY work or craft activities, however, the situation is somewhat different. In these days of high unemployment and economic recession DIY ethusiasts are often tempted to expand their range of activities to include small commercial ventures. These commit the individual, as the manufacturer of the product, to certain legal responsibilities and liabilities. In the event of workmanship or design proving faulty and causing injury, you could be taken to court, for whilst the legislation on product liability, both present and pending, is primarily aimed at larger manufacturers, it is by no means confined to them.

If you are manufacturing goods, or undertaking work for commercial reasons, it may be worth taking advice on your potential liabilities. This book is not intended to be a guide to the law, so take advice from a solicitor or an insurance company. By the same token, if your activities form all, or part, of your paid work, then they may be covered by the Health and Safety at Work Act. Small businesses and companies have always received very little formal attention from the Health and Safety Executive. With the current movement towards self-certification schemes, even that will probably disappear. The fact that nobody is going to call on your workshop in order to check that the machines and so on are safe, does not mean that they are not covered by the law. The Health and Safety at Work Act requires everybody at work, be they employer, employee or self-employed, to look after their own safety and that of people around them. So if you earn a living as a self-employed joiner, and injure yourself on a piece of unsafe equipment, you could be liable to prosecution for failing to ensure your own safety.

Once again, it lies beyond the scope of this book to provide a guide to the law. If you feel that your activities might be covered by the Act, telephone your local Health and Safety Executive for advice.

In such cases you may have to fulfil safety requirements that are much more detailed than those discussed here. Whilst the following rules and guidelines are principally those which are enforced in places of work, they are translated into a form that can be applied easily and sensibly to the home or to the craft workshop; they would not necessarily fulfil the requirements of a Factory Inspector.

# General working conditions

## *Hygiene*

It is always important to work in a clean, well-organised environment. This makes working both safer and easier. Spillages of hazardous liquids, including paints and oils that could be slipped on, must be cleaned up at once. Workshop floors should be non-slip and kept clear of obstructions or rubbish. When decorating, make sure that any sheets or cloths used to cover the floor do not themselves present a slipping hazard. Slips and falls comprise one of the largest single categories of accident, both in the home and at work.

**If irritants or hazardous dusts such as sawdust or ceramic dusts are used in any process, clean the floor with a wet-mop or a commercial vacuum cleaner; this will prevent the dust from re-entering the breathing zone. Do not dry-brush.**

When working with any dusts of this sort, or when using insulating materials for lofts or attics such as spun minerals or glass fibres, hire a commercial vacuum cleaner; the filtering systems of many domestic vacuums are simply not fine enough for this kind of task. The most dangerous particles of any hazardous dust are usually the microscopic ones, for these particles, invisible to the naked eye, pass through the filter of a domestic vacuum cleaner and can be sprayed back into the air. Your local Yellow Pages will contain a list of machinery, equipment and plant hire outlets that will be able to help you.

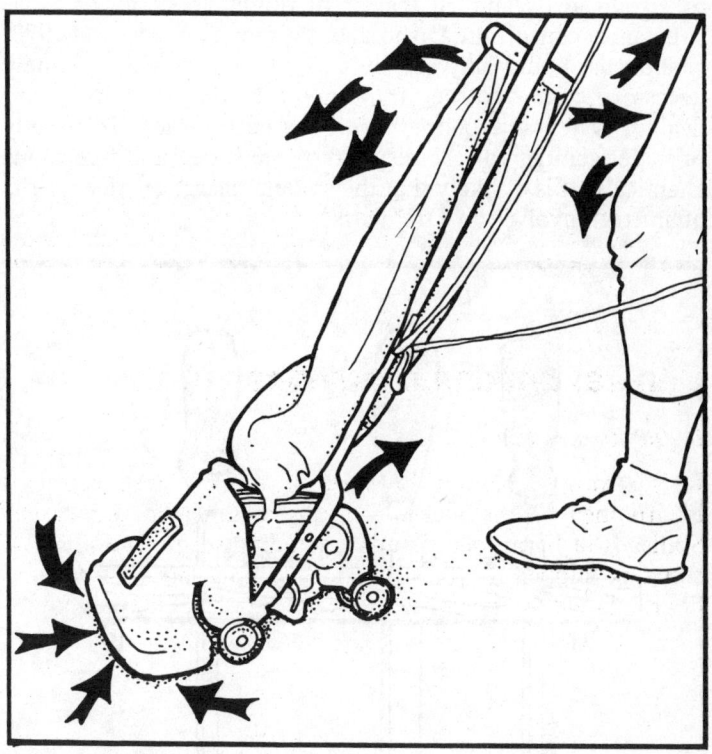

Domestic vacuum cleaners often redistribute fine particles into
the atmosphere

Whatever the work, avoid eating, drinking or smoking in
the vicinity of chemicals or dust for this increases the chance of
accidental ingestion. This rule should also be followed whilst
decorating or building. If you are working inside the home, be
particularly careful to avoid contamination of the living area or
kitchen. In one well-documented case from the United States
two people soldered stained glass in their kitchen and poisoned
their four-year-old son as a result.

The rules outlined in the section on Chemical safety inside
the home apply fully in the workshop, but remember that it is
illegal to pour toxic chemicals down the sink. This also applies

to strong acids and alkalis. If in doubt about a particular substance, consult the Disposal of Poisonous Wastes Act 1972. Chemicals should only be poured down the sink if absolutely necessary, and even then they should be diluted with a good deal of water and poured slowly. Local authorities usually provide facilities for the disposal of unwanted and hazardous chemicals. It is unlikely that they would charge any fee for the quantities involved in DIY work.

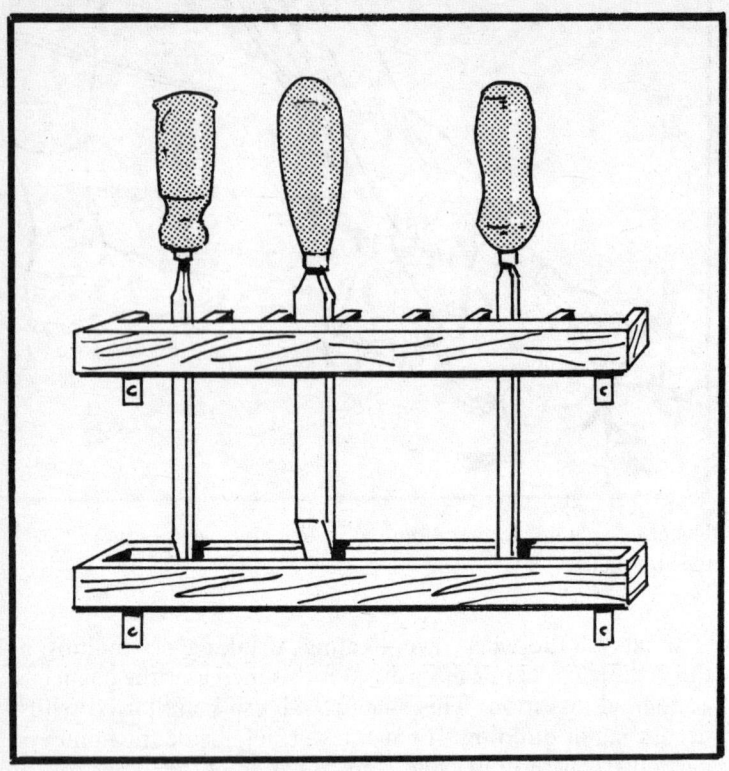

Sharp tools should always be stored away safely

Do not forget that many DIY accidents every year are caused by cutting tools such as chisels and knives. Keep all such tools stored in cupboards or racks. If they have protective sheaths, use them. Wherever possible, remove blades from knives when they are not in use. Do not leave tools lying around unless you are actually using them. Always cut away from your body when you are using chisels or knives, and remember that hand saws, although not sharp in the sense of a chisel or knife, are quite capable of causing an unpleasant cut.

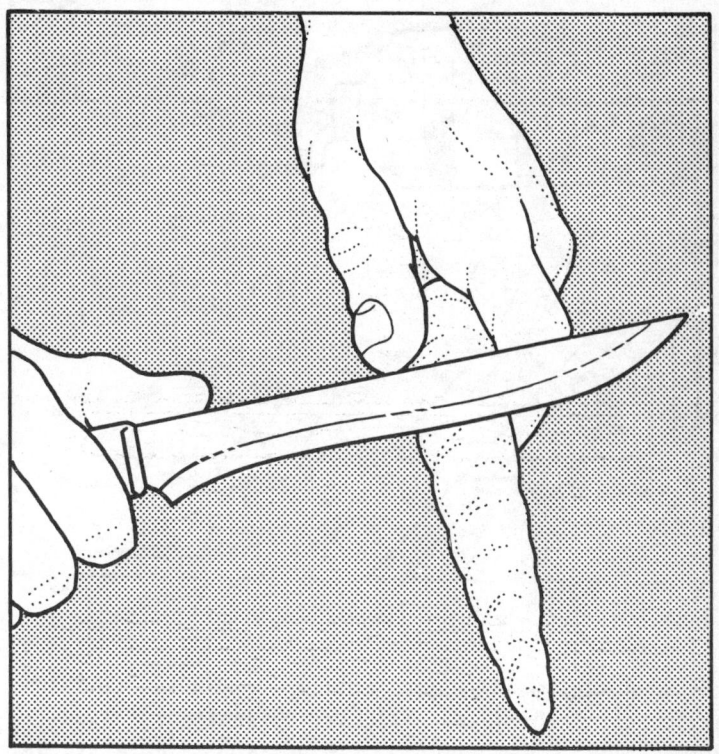

Always cut away from the body when using knives and sharp edges

## Temperature

Studies have shown that accidents happen with greater frequency when the temperature is too low. Do try to maintain a comfortable air temperature, especially when cutting tools or equipment are in use. Precise rules are not as important as

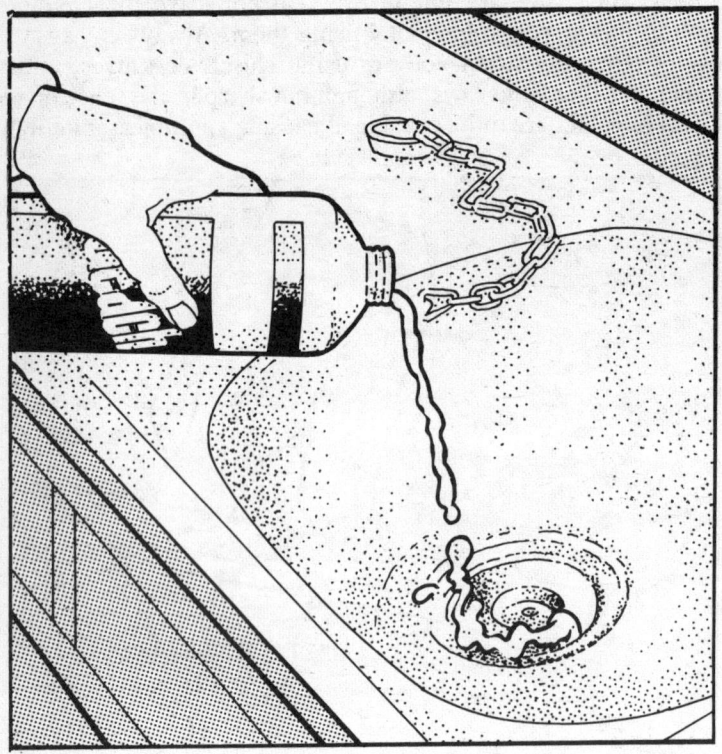

Some chemicals can be disposed of down the sink

personal comfort, but the recommended minimum in industry of 16 degrees centigrade (60.08 degrees fahrenheit) is a good guide. Slightly lower temperatures are acceptable where the work is of a severely physical nature.

## Noise

Noise from machinery can prove irritating and may be a dangerous distraction to you and your neighbours. Minimise it wherever possible. If the noise of a process does cause discomfort wear ear muffs or ear plugs. These can be bought cheaply and easily. Safety equipment suppliers listed in your

Yellow Pages should be able to help you. Early signs of excessive exposure to noise, which can lead to temporary or permanent deafness, include fatigue and nausea.

## Ventilation

If you are using chemicals that emit fumes or vapours, or if you are doing work that creates a lot of dust, then you will need to consider the question of ventilation.

There are two main systems of ventilation: general and local. With general ventilation the air in the working area is replaced so rapidly that the levels of fumes or vapours remain too low to cause damage. This can be achieved with (amongst other things) extractor fans or open windows. Local ventilation is achieved by removing the fumes at their point of creation. This can be done with devices like fume cupboards or extraction booths.

Unless you are regularly using toxic chemicals such as concentrated acids (used in electroplating, glass etching and other processes) or highly-volatile solvents, local ventilation will prove an expensive and largely unnecessary precaution.

Depending upon the nature of the contaminants you encounter, general ventilation should be adequately achieved by opening windows or, weather permitting, by undertaking the work outside. It may, however, be feasible to have an extractor fan installed.

If local ventilation is necessary, then certain points should be remembered. Such systems usually consist of a hood or an enclosure, a duct to remove the contaminated air, and an extractor fan. Should you construct such a system, it is important to enclose the source as effectively as possible; to capture the contaminated air with moving air of adequate velocity; to avoid working between the source of contamination and the hood; to ensure that contaminated air is replaced with clean air; and to discharge contaminated air in such a way that it cannot re-enter the workplace or the living area.

## Lighting

Like temperature and noise, lighting in the DIY workshop is

largely a matter of common sense. A good level of light is essential to safety; this should be both natural *and* artificial if possible.

Remember that certain processes require poor or subdued lighting to be completely safe. Forges and brazing hearths, for instance, should only have subdued lighting; by over-illuminating such areas you may inadvertently disguise the presence of hot metals or substances.

It is a convenient rule of thumb that the finer or more detailed the work, the greater the illumination that will be required. Consequently, a much higher level of illumination will be needed for very detailed engraving than for rough sawing.

**Sometimes people like to attach supplementary illumination to individual machines. Whether this is a bench-mounted lathe or a sewing machine, it is important that the light source be a low-voltage one (between 12V and 24V).**

# Electrical safety

Most DIY power tools are portable, and those that are manufactured now tend to be of the highest possible standards. Many bench-fixed machines are used, however, and the portable tools are often put to uses that create hazards requiring particular consideration.

Machines such as lathes, routers and belt sanders should be stable and securely fixed so that they do not move or vibrate during use. Try to keep a clear space around such machines when they are in operation. The Health and Safety Executive recommends a clear space of at least three feet beyond the maximum length of the material being handled on three sides of the machine. This is evidently going to be impossible in most DIY workshops, but a clear space of some sort should be preserved.

Be careful to switch off all machines when they are not in use, whether they are portable or fixed, and irrespective of how long the machine will be idle.

Keep all machine tools properly stored and well-sharpened. Blunt tools can be more dangerous than sharp ones, as they are more likely to throw up the material being worked. Various devices can be purchased for sharpening tools, including whetstones, and most DIY shops have a tool-sharpening service.

**You must make sure that all machines are safely and properly guarded. With second-hand machines, contact the manufacturer for information about their safe usage and guarding.**

If you have relatively large or dangerous machines in your workshop get a mains circuit breaker fitted, with one or more emergency stop buttons. Make sure that machines are fitted with isolating switches, and that portable tools, especially on long extension leads, are protected by a Residual Current Circuit Breaker (RCCB). If you use any machines that have to be left on overnight, such as ceramic kilns, ensure that they are fitted with a safety cut-off device.

Check that every machine is fitted with control buttons or switches that function properly. Under no circumstances rectify a faulty switch by wiring it to be permanently 'on' and relying upon the wall switch to control the current. If the machine has separate 'on' and 'off' buttons, check that these are the correct colour (green and red respectively).

All machine wiring should be protected with an oil-resistant insulation such as PVC. Insulation, cables and connections must be kept in good condition, and fuses of the correct rating must always be used. It is good practice to set a specific date, perhaps two or three times a year, when you check the wiring on all your equipment in the workshop. Dangerous faults in cables or connections may thus be spotted before trouble occurs.

## Machine guards, power tools, ventilation

Guards on machines fall into four main types: fixed, inter-locked, fixed adjustable and material.

Fixed guards are the most efficient and safe, and should be used wherever possible. Interlocked guards come in various forms, but all function on the same basic principle: when the guard is lifted, the machine can no longer be operated. If a machine is fitted with an interlocking guard, it is important to check that there is a fail-safe device as a back-up to stop the machine should the interlocking mechanism (which switches off the mains current) not function properly.

**Fixed adjustable guards are commonly used on DIY machines and on all machines where constant adjustment is needed. These will not normally require the use of a tool to make an adjustment, but the guard must not under any circumstances be adjusted when the machine is operating.**

Material guards are incorporated with jigs and holders for use only with specific processes or operations. Make sure that the materials used are strong but not too unwieldy.

The use and choice of portable power tools deserves some special mention. Always select the proper tool for the job and never try to force a tool to do something that it was not designed for. Ensure that every tool you buy is fully earthed or double insulated. Avoid extension leads if possible, as the extra length of cable only increases the possibility of electrical faults. Ensure that all bits and blades are kept sharp and clean, and that both they and the tool are kept regularly maintained. Before using a tool always check that the adjusting tool or chuck key has been removed. If you do not do this, the key may be thrown violently from the chuck.

**Never make adjustments to the tool whilst the power is switched on and never leave power tools running whilst they are unattended.**

When using portable power tools, remember that they can be dangerous and use them with common sense. Always read and follow the manufacturer's instructions and make sure that you do not use the tools in such a place that somebody could trip over the flex.

Do not use them in the rain unless they are specifically designed for rough-weather external use. Be careful before drilling or cutting into masonry; check that there are no concealed conduits or power cables that you could sever.

Very occasionally the DIY enthusiast will work in a potentially explosive atmosphere. Heavy fumes from solvents or certain dusts can create such an environment. Under such circumstances, electrical equipment must be considered a potential source of ignition. Operating safely will entail choosing spark or explosion-protected equipment. But the best solution is to avoid the circumstances in the first place by ensuring adequate ventilation.

# Fire hazards

In essence, fire precautions and hazards are the same as those for the home. There are, however, a number of special points to remember, most of which relate to flammable chemicals.

Flammable chemicals encountered in the DIY workshop, or in the garage, include solvents, petroleum, paints, varnishes, adhesives and compressed gases such as Liquefied Petroleum Gases (LPG).

Health and Safety legislation recognises three categories of flammability: Highly Flammable (liquids with a flashpoint of 32 degrees centigrade or below), Flammable (with a flashpoint above 32 degrees centigrade) and petroleum mixtures (those with a flashpoint of 23 degrees centigrade or below are by definition highly flammable).

The 'flashpoint' is a method of expressing the relative flammability of liquids and shows the lowest temperature at which a liquid can give off a mixture of vapour and air which can be ignited by sparks or static electricity. If a liquid is at a lower temperature than its flashpoint the likelihood of ignition is much reduced.

If flammable chemicals are used they should, if possible, be used at a temperature lower than their flashpoint. When assessing whether a dangerous concentration of fumes is present, consider the liquid's properties and conditions of usage. For instance, vaporised liquids used as a spray may still be ignited at a temperature lower than their flashpoint if the ignition source is hot enough.

If your DIY work involves regular usage of flammable liquids then cleanliness will be of particular importance. Workplaces where highly flammable deposits accumulate should be cleaned at frequent intervals – perhaps even every week. If you are spraying highly-flammable materials, try to use clean, dry filters for each different substance. This reduces the possibility of spontaneous combustion of interacting chemicals.

**Spontaneous combustion can occur with a number of different materials. Typical examples include lacquers**

containing nitrocellulose combined with finishers such as varnishes which contain drying oils, and oxidising agents with any organic material.

Many plastics are potentially flammable, either individually or in combination. Try to check with the manufacturer before use, or use the 'scissors test' mentioned elsewhere, and attempt to ignite a small sample in the open air.

Any cloth, rag or material soaked in a flammable liquid such as turpentine, turpentine substitute (white spirit) or paraffin should be disposed of. The best way to do this is by controlled burning. Make sure this is done outdoors and at least twenty feet away from any building, hedge, tree or construction. When you are doing this be careful not to stand over the flames as the fumes may be dangerous.

Fire fighting methods have already been discussed in the section on Fire safety. Keeping fire extinguishers in the workshop and garage is a sensible precaution, but analyse carefully the sorts of burning materials that you are likely to encounter. Paper, wood and rags are best tackled with a water-based extinguisher; in the workshop these have the advantage over dry powder extinguishers that they can be used effectively against blow torches and gas cylinders. In the garage where burning liquids such as oil or petrol are more likely to be present, a halon (BCF) extinguisher could be more suitable.

It is worth noting in passing that many public service vehicles, such as ambulances and buses, are provided with halon extinguishers because of their effectiveness in fighting burning liquids. Extinguishers sold for cars tend to be too small, and dry powder based – which is not the best material. When selecting an extinguisher for a car it might be sensible to choose a small (about 1 kg) halon-based model. Whilst this will be somewhat more expensive and more heavy than a conventional type, its effectiveness on burning vehicles is such as to justify its purchase. Remember equally, however, that halon is only of limited use on burning solids.

Anyone using or storing highly flammable chemicals in a workshop or outbuilding would be well advised to contact the fire brigade. Ultimately, fire precautions depend upon the particular circumstances under which the material is being used. They will arrange for a Fire Prevention Officer (FPO) to make a visit, and to give more specific advice if it is needed.

# Chemical safety

Some categories of hazardous chemicals found in or around the home are specific to the DIY workshop. In general terms these can be divided into adhesives, solvents and compressed gases.

## *Adhesives*

When using adhesives, always wear suitable protective clothing, ensure adequate ventilation, and avoid smoking, eating or drinking in the vicinity. Do not permit any playing around with modern adhesives, especially the instant bond 'superglue' type. When using this sort of glue be especially careful to wear gloves and to avoid splashing. Although its effects have been somewhat exaggerated, it must be treated with caution. Bonded skin should be freed with warm, soapy water. If this is not effective, do not attempt to cut yourself free, but seek medical advice.

The main hazards associated with solvent-borne adhesives arise from the solvents themselves. The same is true of their respective thinners and cleaners.

Some water-borne adhesives can prove dermatitic so avoid skin contact. Wear gloves and overalls if using them in considerable quantities, and wash splashes from the skin with water. If splashed in the eyes, mouth or nose, wash immediately and seek medical advice. Water-borne adhesives are used, amongst other things, for bonding wood.

The main hazard arising from hot-melt adhesives is the heat, with temperatures of over 200 degrees centigrade sometimes used. Avoid any skin contact and wear protective clothing. If skin contact does occur, cool the adhesive with water and apply a cold compress. Seek medical advice and do not attempt to remove the glue.

**Ventilation is important, for if the adhesive catches fire it**

**will release toxic, black smoke. Old adhesive is more likely to
burst into flames than fresh, because its 'auto-ignition'
temperature is lower. It is therefore important to avoid storing
unused adhesive for too long.**

Chemically-reactive adhesives usually have two ingredients to
be mixed together, the 'adhesive' or epoxide and a catalyst or
'hardener'. Skin contact with or inhalation of epoxide glues must
be avoided. Certain hardeners have been known to cause asthma.

Two-part acrylic adhesives are also chemically-reactive, and are
both irritant and highly-flammable. To make them even less
desirable, they emit an extremely unpleasant, nauseous odour.

Many chemically-reactive adhesives contain materials that are
dermatitic or that cause skin sensitisation. Splashes or smears of
the adhesive or its components on the skin should be removed
with a paper tissue and the affected area washed thoroughly with
soapy water.

Some adhesives come in powder form; these can sometimes be
dermatitic and may also present a respiratory hazard. Adequate
ventilation is therefore important, as is avoiding skin contact.
Remember that fine dusts may be potentially explosive so avoid
stirring up the dust when mixing the adhesive and do not expose
the dust to a naked flame.

Cement-based adhesives (including cement itself) are alkaline
once they are mixed with water and are capable of causing limited
burns of the skin. Lime in its pure form is even more dangerous.
Always wear PVC gloves when mixing cement or handling wet
cement compounds.

## Solvents

Solvents are among the most common DIY chemicals of a
potentially dangerous character and are used in adhesives,
thinners, paints, lacquers, varnishes and in a variety of other
products.

Although some solvents are dermatitic, it is the effect of
their vapours on the body that poses the most serious threat.
This is because they are able to dissolve body fats, and because
they tend to vaporise at low temperatures. Liver and kidney
damage are common effects of long-term exposure to solvents,
whilst short-term exposure can produce a narcotic effect

(as in solvent abuse, or 'glue-sniffing').

**Certain prescribed drugs affect the liver's ability to deal with toxic chemicals and will lead to an increased sensitivity to the narcotic effects of solvents. People taking drugs such as sleeping tablets or tranquillisers should avoid contact with solvents or their vapours wherever possible.**

Solvents may be sold under a confusing variety of trade names, although the basic chemical and hazards are the same. Hydrocarbons are one of the most common groups of solvents, and include gasoline, greases, kerosene, paraffin wax, petroleum ether, benzene, napthalene, toluene and xylene.

Alcohols and acetates (or esters) are also solvents ('substituted hydrocarbons'). Other familiar solvents or solvent-based products include carbon tetrachloride (dry-cleaning fluid), acetone, acrolein, camphor, fused oils, lacquers, varnishes, shellac, turpentine and turpentine substitute (white spirit).

Precautions when using these are generally the same: avoid inhalation, ensure adequate ventilation and wash skin and clothes regularly. A good (though somewhat unrealistic) test is to consider your ventilation inadequate if you can smell the solvent that you are using. Remember also that solvents tend to be highly flammable so must not be exposed to heat or naked flames.

## Compressed gases

Oxygen, acetylene and, occasionally, compressed air are the gases most likely to be encountered in the DIY workshop. These gases are supplied, like fire extinguishers or their labels, in different coloured cylinders to avoid confusion. Oxygen cylinders are black, acetylene maroon and compressed air grey.

Never attempt to mix gases in a cylinder or fill one cylinder from another. Handle cylinders with care and do not bump or bang them. Keep cylinders away from electrical equipment or processes and make sure that hands and gloves are grease-free before attempting to lift them. Keep cylinder valves clean. Clear dirt from the valve sockets by briefly opening and closing the cylinder valve before fitting the regulator. Dirt in the cylinder valve socket may cause leakage to occur. Never leave cylinders unattended without shutting their valves. Always shut the valve when the cylinder is empty. Never lubricate valves or use white or red lead jointing compound.

**If you think a cylinder is leaking use soapy water, not a naked flame, to test it. Thaw out frozen valves with hot water, not a flame or blow torch.**

If using oxygen and acetylene (oxyacetylene) to weld or cut metal, fit an automatic pressure regulator to the cylinders. Needle valves should not be relied on as they will not prevent a back flow of gases to the cylinder and will put the hose under full cylinder pressure. Check hoses and fittings regularly. Remember that the shorter the hose, the less chance there is of it leaking. Use red hoses for acetylene, and blue for oxygen.

Store oxygen and acetylene cylinders separately. Oxygen can be stored horizontally, in which case it is a good idea to put wedges under the cylinders to stop them rolling, but acetylene must be stored upright. Protect cylinders from extremes of temperature. If storing them outside, cover them with something to provide shade from the sun. Do not allow the cover to touch the cylinders and avoid lying them on wet soil.

If you have any enquiries, or if you discover a faulty or damaged cylinder, contact the supplier or manufacturer immediately. Never take a risk and use a faulty or damaged cylinder, nor leave it near a heat source, or near full cylinders.

Each different type of gas presents its own hazards and requires individual attention.

Oxygen is a non-flammable and odourless gas. However, its presence is essential for most forms of combustion and it will greatly increase the ferocity of a fire. Likewise, a fire is more likely to start in an oxygen-rich atmosphere. For this reason it is important to avoid releasing oxygen in confined areas or near naked flames.

Acetylene is an extremely dangerous gas and must be used with great caution. It is highly flammable and has a strong smell. Stray sparks or hot metal will instantly ignite acetylene, which is also capable of forming explosive compounds with certain metals, including copper and silver. Because of this, copper fittings or piping must never be used with acetylene.

**If an acetylene cylinder is accidently heated, emergency action must be taken. Shut the valve and detach the regulator.**

**Remove the cylinder to the open air and cool it with water. If it is safe to do so, open the valve and release all the gas. If it is not safe to do this, call the fire brigade.**

Compressed air is used to power spray guns and pneumatic tools, and to clean work surfaces. Whether it is supplied from a cylinder or from a small compressor, the pressure is dangerous. Under no circumstances use compressed air to blow dust or wood shavings from clothing. Never point an air line or spray gun at either your own or somebody else's body. Never engage in 'horseplay' with compressed air. 'Goosing' people with compressed air lines has been known to cause the most devastating injuries.

Always connect the spray gun or tool before turning on the air supply. Failure to do this will make the air line whip violently.

Make sure that all hose connections are tight and not blocked or damaged. Remember to turn off the air before loosening a connection. Always check that safety valves on compressors are working before switching on. This is especially important if the compressor has previously been damaged.

Receivers must be high quality, strong and made of good material. Never improvise or use home-made receivers. Never use a compressor with a faulty pressure gauge; a build-up of pressure may cause a receiver to explode.

# Lifting and carrying

According to the 1984 HASS report, 'over exertion' (including strain injuries caused by carrying heavy weights) only accounted for 0.8 per cent of the total number of injuries (883 out of 110,254). However, this gives a slightly misleading indication of the dangers of lifting weights as it does not include the number of people who go to their GP, or who simply take to their beds for a few days.

In industry the dangers of lifting and carrying heavy weights are well established and a clearly defined code for doing both has been devised. Try to follow this whenever lifting heavy things.

Lifting heavy weights can cause back injuries; always follow the
correct procedure

## Lifting

1. Crouch down to the object that you want to lift. Do not
stand with straight legs and bend your back to reach down.
Keep your legs apart.
2. Try to position one foot alongside the object, with the other
one slightly to the rear.
3. Grip the object firmly, holding with the palms of your hands
and the roots of your fingers.
4. Keep your back straight and lift using your legs and leg
muscles. Use the rearmost foot to push-off with and try to do

this in the direction required in one single, smooth movement.

## Carrying

1. Keep the load in such a position that you can see clearly in front of you and try to keep your arms close to your body.
2. Be careful to avoid pinching or trapping your fingers when pushing the load down.

Before attempting to lift a heavy weight do remember that this could strain the heart and possibly even prove fatal. If you are in any doubt about your ability to easily lift the object that you want to move, get somebody to help you, or set up a block-and-tackle or lifting rig.

# Personal protection

There are a number of different DIY processes where personal protection of some sort is necessary: chipping or cutting stone, milling or grinding tools, or laying-down loft insulation are just a few examples.

## Eyes

The eyes must always be protected when the work in hand involves any risk of corrosive or irritant liquids splashing, of chips or sparks flying, or of tools or other materials being thrown up.

For grinding, chipping or drilling, there are three fundamental forms of eye protection: spectacles with impact-resistant lenses, flexible or cushioned goggles and chipping or eye-cup goggles. All of these can be purchased easily and relatively cheaply. Buy only those that conform to BS 2092.

Protection against splashes of hazardous liquids is best provided by face shields or complete acid hoods which cover all exposed skin, but tight-fitting goggles will do if necessary.

When welding you will require a mask that both covers your entire face and contains the correct filter to protect your eyes

Wear the correct eye protection if a process involves sparks or chippings

from the intense light which is generated. Do not forget that it is not only visible light, but also infra-red and ultraviolet light that is produced.

## Hands

During a lot of DIY work the hands are the part of the body most likely to be at risk. Take extra care whenever cutting with sharp edges or tools and when using machinery. Avoid unnecessary contact with chemicals of any sort. Gloves are absolutely essential to prevent both short- and long-term problems including chemical burns, dermatitis and sensitisation. Sensitisation of the skin is a complaint where long-term exposure to a chemical, although it may not immediately cause damage, creates an allergy that can sometimes produce symptoms like dermatitis.

Different activities and processes require different types of glove. Ordinary gardening gloves, with or without a suede palm, are fine for work where the hands are likely to become dirty or cold, but they do not offer protection against heat, crushing or chemicals. The suede palm, however, does offer some protection against glass or other sharp objects in the soil, so their use is strongly recommended.

Chrome-tanned leather gloves should be used for processes involving intense heat, sparks or chippings. Do not use asbestos gloves as these sometimes decompose when they wear out, releasing deadly fibres into the atmosphere.

If machinery or cutting-tools are likely to present a hazard, try to get metal mesh gloves. These have a metal reinforcement specifically designed to turn back cutting blades.

Gloves which are meant to provide protection against chemicals are invariably made of plastic or rubber. Different types are suited to specific chemicals. If you are using any toxic chemicals on a regular basis you should select your gloves carefully.

Natural rubber or latex gloves are only to be recommended for use with dilute acids and alkalis. Gloves made from neoprene rubber will protect against a wider range of chemicals, including dilute and concentrated acids, alkalis, paint thinners, petroleum distillates and turpentine. They are also the only glove type recommended for use with polyester resins, which are used to reinforce the fabric in glass fibre work. Using the correct gloves when working with glass fibre (or GRP, Glass Reinforced Plastic) is important as both the resins and the catalysts can be harmful.

For many people, Polyvinyl Chloride (PVC) will be the most accessible glove type. However, before embarking on any major projects with PVC gloves as protection do remember that, whilst they are recommended for use with dilute acids and alkalis, they are not really suitable for concentrated acids, lacquer thinners, paint or varnish removers, paint thinners, petroleum distillates, polyester resins or turpentine.

Safety equipment suppliers (see your local Yellow Pages)

will be able to provide most of these glove types. Keep the insides of any gloves you buy clear of contamination and wash the outsides regularly. This will both ensure cleanliness, and prolong the life of the glove.

Barrier creams are quite easy to obtain and use, but are not as efficient as gloves and should, therefore, only be used in conjunction with gloves. Some chemicals will combine with barrier creams and increase the risk of skin irritations. Apply barrier creams before starting work, and on to dry, clean skin.

## General protection

Sometimes more general protection is necessary. With any activity that involves the risk of contamination wear overalls, a 'bib-and-brace' or a lab coat; processes where this is necessary include painting and decorating, car maintenance, stripping furniture, and activities which produce dust or fibres, such as ceramics work, loft insulation or glass fibre work.

Choose clothing which is loose enough to fit over your day-to-day clothes and which is made from a tightly-woven fabric. Wash these clothes regularly and rinse them out well. If possible, avoid washing contaminated clothing with the rest of your laundry.

Certain specific processes require special mention. A leather apron should be worn whilst welding; this will protect against burns to the body or clothing, and in the case of gas-shielded welding processes will also help to avoid the effects of ultraviolet radiation. A leather apron is particularly important when operating from a sitting position.

Some people use home foundries to cast in metals such as aluminium and bronze. This work involves pouring molten metal and so spats or gaiters, a leather or heat-resistant apron, a high-impact visor and heat-resistant gloves should always be worn. Under no circumstances wear man-made fabrics such as nylon – these can melt into the skin on contact with a heat source.

Where work involves hazardous chemicals wear a flame-resistant or cloth apron if lab coats or overalls are not available.

## Breathing

Inhalation is one of the more common routes of poisoning. There are two types of respirators available that will offer some protection against this: air purifying (like the old-fashioned gas masks) and air supplying. Respirators of any sort should only ever be a final precaution and not a substitute for adequate ventilation or good hygiene and working practice.

Check that your respirator is a good fit. Cover the air outlet whilst you are wearing it and breathe in; you should not notice any air leaking in around the chin or nose. Repeat with the exhaust covered, breathing out. You should not have to over-tighten the straps to ensure a good fit. If you are doing work where a respirator is necessary, which ideally includes anything that produces fibre or dust such as work involving fibre glass, grinding or cutting ceramics, stone or bricks, and laying spun-mineral insulation, it is important that it fits tightly. All respirators have limited effectiveness over long periods, especially if they do not fit well.

All respirators should be regularly cleaned and maintained. With the more elaborate types this will probably mean that a professional service is necessary.

Air-purifying respirators consist of a face mask, and a filter which removes any contamination from the air you breathe. If you buy one, check that the filter is the correct one for the chemical in use and purchase a good supply so that you can change the filter frequently.

Air-supplying respirators use compressed gas cylinders, compressor units or self-contained breathing equipment to supply the user with uncontaminated air. It is unlikely that the DIY enthusiast will deal with chemicals quite so toxic that they require such elaborate and expensive precautions; if they are felt to be necessary for a particular process, it would be wiser to substitute a less-hazardous process than to invest large sums of money in breathing apparatus.

Cheap paper and cloth masks (or 'smog masks') are not a reliable form of protection against toxic hazards and should only be used against large particle or fibre nuisance dusts.

# Storage

Store DIY chemicals out of the reach of children and pets. The best place is in a locked outbuilding or workshop. Take similar precautions with sharp or otherwise dangerous tools.

**Where corrosive or toxic chemicals are concerned, inspect both their containers and shelves or racks regularly. In particular, look for rust or, in the case of wooden shelves, signs of rot or collapse. Do not design your shelves so that you have to stretch to reach them.**

Keep chemicals cool and dry, but above their freezing point. If this requires the use of a fridge, buy a separate one just for that purpose – never put both food and chemicals in the same storage area. Chemicals which might require this include some highly-volatile solvents and some professional photographic products. High-quality reconditioned fridges can be bought easily and cheaply.

Try not to 'jumble' different substances on the shelves. Keep paints together in one area, solvents and thinners in another, oils in a third, and so on. Quite apart from reducing the possibility of chemical spillages reacting together, this makes it easier for you to find what you want.

Liquefied petroleum gas (LPG) cylinders such as butane and propane should be stored in an upright position outside or in a fire-proof enclosure. Always observe this even when camping or caravaning – LPG has caused a number of serious accidents and can be quite unstable under certain conditions. Try to keep cylinders out of both sun and rain if possible.

**Oxygen and fuel gas cylinders should be stored away from oil and grease, with which they can react violently.**

Remember – if you are in doubt about the correct way to store any chemical contact either your Fire Prevention Officer at the local fire station, or the manufacturer. The manufacturer has an obligation to make certain information about the chemical available to you.

# DIY AND CRAFT PROCESSES

There are a number of specialised DIY and craft processes that are practiced by sufficiently large numbers of people to merit closer examination; if your hobby or activity is not included amongst these you should consult the organisations listed at the end of this book to discover which extra precautions, if any, you should take.

## Ceramics

Pottery is a popular subject at evening classes, illustrating people's continuing interest in one of the oldest practical skills.

Very few people in Britain construct their own ceramics studios and kilns at home; most of the thousands of enthusiastic potters are either students or are attending classes in their local art college or night school.

It would be nice to be able to assume that such institutions follow health and safety guidelines precisely; sadly, the truth is often the reverse. If you are planning to develop a practical interest in ceramics, whether at home, in a studio or in night school, you will probably have to assume some responsibility for your own safety. This will sometimes appear to be in direct conflict with the accepted practice in your working environment. The responsibility to resolve such conflicts, and to look after personal safety, lies entirely with yourself.

It is worth noting that if you are a student, or are attending evening classes at a college or local school, then you are covered by the Health and Safety at Work Act etc 1974. Your tutors, assuming they are paid, are in their place of work, and you count as a person other than an employee in that workplace.

This means that it would be quite proper for you to insist that all reasonable steps are taken to protect your personal safety. The person responsible for your welfare will be your supervisor, whether they are a tutor or a technical assistant.

## Hygiene

Poisoning is the main hazard of ceramics work, whether from silica dust or from the list of toxic chemicals used for glazing. If working at home, try to arrange your workshop so that you can clean it with a wet mop. This will dampen down clay dust, which contains a high level of silica. A dry brush would stir the dust up again.

**By breathing appreciable quantities of silica dust you may develop silicosis, an extremely serious and sometimes fatal chest disease.**

A number of processes produce localised dust (high levels of dust in the immediate vicinity of the work being done). This is especially likely in areas where clay is being prepared, and where tile presses are functioning. It is very important to ensure adequate dust extraction or ventilation in these areas, and to wear a face mask. If at all possible, any work that produces dust should be done in an extraction cubicle which has an exhaust to the outside atmosphere. Clay dust accumulates extremely quickly, so the working area should be cleaned every time it has been used. Occasionally wash walls and ceilings as well.

Avoid dusty overalls. Keep all working clothes clean and choose a material such as terylene, which retains less dust than cotton or wool.

With glazes, which often contain a variety of hazardous dusts, add the materials to water before mixing. Carefully pour the dry material into the middle of the water, disturbing as little dust as possible.

Cover any working surfaces with an impervious (non-absorbent) material such as formica and clean them regularly. Clean the undersides of benches and tables and do not work on untreated wooden surfaces.

If possible, avoid using flint or quartz as a 'placing' medium in your kiln; both constitute a major dust hazard once they have been heated and aired. A number of non-toxic alternatives, including aluminium hydrates, are commercially available.

## Chemical safety

In addition to the dangers presented by silica or silica-bearing dusts, there are a number of toxic or harmful chemicals in the potter's workplace.

The preparation and use of glazes brings the greatest risk of poisoning, especially when materials such as chromium or free silica (in the form of ground flint or quartz) are involved. It is important to minimise skin contact with glazes in general and to ensure a high level of personal hygiene. Wear gloves and barrier creams if prolonged contact with solutions such as glazes or slips (thin mixes of water and clay) is necessary. Wash your hands thoroughly after any work, paying particular attention to the finger nails.

If supervisors do not provide information on the ingredients and comparative toxicity of the different glazes in use, and if this information is not provided by the labels of bottles you use when working at home, then you will need to identify these for yourself. Always substitute less hazardous glazes wherever possible.

One major concern in ceramics work intended for use as crockery or cooking utensils is the likelihood that chemicals may escape from the glaze and poison the user. This is of importance to anyone making pots. The chemical reactions that occur when glazes are fired, and the effects of mixing different glazes together, form a huge area of study and reference. Before embarking of any project where the finished product will be used as an eating, drinking or cooking utensil, obtain a good book on the subject and avoid the temptation to experiment.

Lead is a commonly encountered hazard in both ceramics and glass work. Its poisonous properties as a solid (in fishing weights) and in fumes (from car exhausts in the United Kingdom) have been widely publicised, yet people still paint children's toys with lead-based paints and poison themselves with the fumes from kilns and furnaces. Be careful when working with lead and follow all the rules.

**Never use raw lead compounds in a glaze; instead use lead 'frits'. Frits are melted or fused separately before being added to the glaze. Lead compounds cannot be made completely insoluble by just fritting but it does make them much less volatile when they are fired.**

Do not use lead frits in glazes which are going to be fired at temperatures exceeding 1,170 degrees centigrade, as they will become highly unpredictable at this point. Also, do not use them for 'raku' glazes on crockery or cooking utensils as the firing process is inconsistent and the temperature too low to ensure a safe finish. Note that lead frits do not guarantee a safe glaze. You must study variables such as the ratio of ingredients, the thickness of the glaze, the length and temperature of firing, and the kiln atmosphere before you can assess the quantity of lead that a glaze might release.

If glazes are mixed, the amount of lead within the ratio of ingredients must be meticulously checked again. Do not add copper to any lead glaze that is going to be used for kitchen or functional ware as it will increase the amount of lead that can be released.

Remember that glazes sometimes break down and release fumes when they are fired. Typical of these are Cornish stone, which releases fluorine gas, wood ash which (if not thoroughly washed) releases sulphur dioxide, and enamel lustres, which release acrid fumes during the early stages of firing.

Glazes that are sprayed on should only be used in a spray booth or hood. Make sure that the booth has a fine particle filter; the spray will pass through anything coarser.

**Applying glazes by the vapour technique is a dangerous operation and must only be carried out if you are experienced, or have professional supervision. This process releases toxic gases such as chlorine and hydrogen chloride and must only be undertaken with adequate extraction equipment attached to a kiln in a separate building.**

Check the chemical content and hazards of ceramic colourants. As always, contact the manufacturer or supplier for advice if this information is not clear. Different stains are applied in different ways and present different hazards.

'Body' stains use fine powders, which must be extracted efficiently, and soluble salts when in the 'slop' state. 'Glaze' stains also present a dry powder and soluble salt risk. Be careful when adding glaze stains to ensure that they do not alter the resistance of the glaze to acids and alkalis.

'Under-glaze' colours sometimes contain lead in the flux – check this. They also present a dry powder risk. 'In-glaze' colours are usually low-temperature enamels containing lead in their flux. The flux is sometimes soluble making it highly unsuitable for functional ware.

With all these stains, be extremely careful to avoid accidentally eating, drinking or inhaling the compounds. Pay particular attention to personal hygiene.

With ceramic inks, avoid disturbing the dust, as the resin in it is potentially explosive if it forms a fine enough mist. Resins of this sort produce dangerous, acrid fumes if they catch fire. Ceramic ink resins are dissolved in solvents, which must themselves be treated with care.

## Machinery and equipment

Ceramics equipment tends to be extremely heavy, expensive and noisy, so it is unlikely that many people will install it as part of a home pottery set-up. It is more likely that this equipment will be encountered in the college or night class, in which case it should, by law, be properly guarded and marked with warning signs and its use should be properly supervised. However, education cuts and the resultant under-staffing in many colleges mean that supervision is not always as rigorous as it might be and that the equipment is not as new or as safe as would be ideal. Furthermore, one or two of the guards for machines such as pugmills actually hamper the machine's function and are sometimes left off.

Blungers and mixers are extremely dangerous machines and should only be used by properly trained staff. All moving parts must be guarded and the feed entrance fitted with a chute or hopper. Note that second-hand industrial dough mixers are occasionally acquired from bakers as cheap alternatives; in such cases it is essential that the Health and Safety Executive is consulted for advice.

If you build your own kiln place it in a separate area with its own exhaust flue and canopy. The HSE should be able to offer some advice about the location and accessibility of kilns, but make sure that your kiln is outside the home. Before operating it, have its siting checked and approved by your local Fire Prevention Officer.

Building your own kiln is not as uncommon or eccentric as it might seem, so do not rush into it with an adventurous spirit supported only by a thumbnail sketch from the local art college. There are a number of good and thorough books available on the subject – so get one. Constructing a kiln requires a lot of work and investment; both this and your safety could be jeopardised if it is not done properly. Most kiln fires are the result of faulty flashing around the kiln chimney so have this constructed professionally. Keep a fire extinguisher near the kiln. Fit the kiln with heat fuses to ensure that it does not exceed its maximum temperature and with a cut-off type pyrometer to regulate its working temperature.

**The kiln chimney must be separated from roof timbers and construction by a gap of at least eight inches, and it must be possible for air to circulate freely around the chimney to keep it cool during firing.**

Electrically-operated kilns require particularly stringent safety mechanisms and must be approved by the electricity board. Note that kilns for raku or salt glaze firing should be constructed out-of-doors inside a covered shelter.

Do not attempt to install a gas-fired kiln unless you are a competent, qualified gas engineer. Even then, the finished work must be approved by British Gas.

Igniting gas kilns is sometimes hazardous; if a sufficient volume of gas/air mixture exists it will explode. Ensure that the kiln is fitted with a safety cut-out device (similar to that in a gas oven) which will not allow gas to enter the kiln unless an ignition source is there.

Complete combustion is important because unused gas could otherwise enter the flue system and could possibly explode. If you use forced-air burners with a manual ignition system, design observation holes so that a clear and safe view of the burner is possible. If ignition does not occur within ten seconds, or less if the manufacturers recommend it, turn off the gas and let the kiln clear before attempting to light it again.

Gas kilns should be fitted with a flame detection safeguard system; the three main systems are flame conduction, flame rectification, and radiation detection. Consult the manufacturers for advice on the most suitable system for your design of kiln.

Manufacturers will supply line diagrams with gas or oil fired kilns. These show the correct system for the layout of pipes and valve mechanisms. Ensure that these instructions are followed exactly.

Wear face protection when viewing the interior of a hot kiln. This is particularly important when reduction firing as a tongue of flame can leap from the inspection hole when the cover or bung is removed. Do not open a kiln until it has cooled to below 250 degrees centigrade. Avoid handling any pots until you are sure they have cooled down.

With lathes, a guard should prevent access to the point where the belt runs into the pulley – do not remove this whilst the machine is operating. Never change the belt to a different set of pulleys (to alter the running speed) unless the machine is switched off at the mains.

Pottery wheels are almost certainly one of the most familiar ceramics machines (remember the old BBC intermission film?). Any exposed pulleys and belts should be guarded. The only real hazard is that of water on electrically-operated wheels. Double-check the earthing and only use sealed-unit switches which are designed to come into contact with liquids. Long hair or clothing must be kept away from moving parts.

Pugmills, like blungers and mixers, must be used by trained people only. Fundamentally, a pugmill is a powerful screw contained in a casing. As clay is fed into the machine, it is squirted through a tiny hole at the bottom or side; this action forces any air bubbles out of the clay. Ideally, pugmills should be fitted with bar guards to prevent access to the screw. If this is not possible then they should be fitted with an extension hopper. Keep all long hair and loose clothing away from the mechanism and familiarise yourself with the position of both the machine's switches and any wall mounted emergency switches.

# Glass work

Skills involving hot and cold glass work are enjoying a revival in both the arts and the crafts. However the availability of non-industrial facilities for hot glass work is extremely limited, with the result that activities such as glass blowing tend to be the exclusive domain of professional artists and craftspeople, and not something that the amateur can easily enjoy access to. Also, because the inherent dangers of blowing shapes in molten glass at temperatures of up to 1,500 degrees centigrade are obvious, safety is usually a high-priority consideration in such processes, and therefore does not require elaboration in a general book such as this.

## Cold glass work

It is cold glass work that is of particular importance here. Broadly speaking, this covers any activities involving cutting, grinding, polishing, etching, and stained glass.

Broken or cut glass has razor sharp edges, something attested to by the fact that glass featured in 1.4 per cent of all the accidents studied in the 1984 HASS report (1,537 accidents out of a total of 110,254). Always treat glass with great caution. Whether fitting window panes or constructing a stained-glass lampshade, handle and carry the glass carefully. Do not leave glass lying around. If panes of glass are left, even if only briefly, take the time to place something on or over them to increase their visibility.

**Never carry glass up ladders. If an upper floor window is broken, either work from the inside (by removing the frame if necesssary) or work with assistance from somebody on the inside.**

If glass has to be transported, tape the panes face to face and wrap them in cloth or layers of brown paper. If possible, place the panes between slightly larger sheets of hardboard and seal the edges with tape or carry the package in an artist's portfolio.

150

## Cutting glass

Whenever cutting glass, wear either metal mesh or stout leather gloves. After scoring with the glass cutter, break the unwanted piece off with the body of the glass resting on a flat surface; under no circumstances hold the pane between both hands and attempt to break it by flexing. Small pieces of glass should be broken off with grozing irons or pliers, but not with your fingers. Cover the jaws of pliers with a piece of cloth to prevent them from splintering or powdering the glass.

Always keep a bin nearby in which to throw offcuts and splinters. Do not keep fragments of stained glass in open boxes, bags or on shelves, but instead store them in flat drawers or in boxes with lids. Never throw broken glass into the dustbin; securely wrap it in paper inside a sealed bag or box to protect the refuse collector.

Do not permit children or pets to play in the vicinity of your work.

## Grinding and polishing

Grinding wheels must run true and at the speed recommended by the manufacturer. Do not use wheels that have become worn near their boresize or that have been cracked.

Protect electrical switches and motors from water, especially since machine cutting, grinding and polishing tend to be wet processes. Use plenty of water, for this will be needed to cool the wheels, damp-down the dust and wash away the waste. If you do not use enough the glass may shatter whilst you are working on it. Polishing wheels, which are usually made of felt, cork or wood, can generate a great deal of heat, so they must always be wet and the glass must be kept on the move.

If using a clay-trap system for collecting waste, be careful to wash away the resulting mixture of glass, corundum and pummice with plenty of water as it is inclined to set like concrete in the drains.

**Do not try to retrieve anything that has fallen into the water tub whilst the wheels are moving. Switch off the**

**machine and wait until the wheels have stopped before putting your hand in.**

When emptying water tubs, decant them slowly after the slurry has settled. Any glass dust or grinding and polishing agents left behind can be washed away with water.

## Stained glass

Apart from the hazards of cutting explained above, the main dangers from working with stained glass stem from the presence of lead in the solders and acid in the flux. Solders are more likely to release lead if they are overheated. Because the 'copper foil' technique uses more solder than the 'lead came' technique it is more likely to cause a lead hazard. Cutting or sanding lead came produces hazardous dust so do not eat or drink in the work area. Acid fluxes can give off irritant fumes and burn the skin, so they should only be used where there is adequate ventilation. Some colourants used to decorate the glass may contain toxic chemicals such as copper sulphate, antimony chloride, silver nitrate or selenium dioxide; treat these with care.

## Etching

Etching glass is a specialised and hazardous process, although it is surprisingly popular. The main element of risk is the acid itself: hydrofluoric acid, which is used to dissolve glass.

Always keep a large container of sodium bicarbonate alongside the workbench. In the event of somebody splashing themselves the affected area can be neutralised by immersion in the alkaline solution.

Before commencing work, coat the bench with whiting solution. Wear heavy-duty rubber gloves, a rubber apron and wellington boots, and protect your eyes with goggles. Sprinkle whiting on your hands before putting on the gloves.

It is a good idea to stain the acid a distinctive colour with a suitable dye; your supplier or manufacturer should be able to suggest a recipe for doing this. The coloured acid will then not be easily confused with other liquids in the work area.

Like most acids, hydrogen fluoride gives off fumes. It is important to ensure a high level of ventilation and extraction whilst working.

# Metalworking

Although metal is not as commonly used in DIY and craft work as wood, processes which are sometimes encountered include forging, welding, soldering, casting and some machine work.

## Forging

The recommendations for ceramic kilns apply to forging as well; stringent fire precautions must be observed at all times and professional advice on construction and maintenance must be both sought and followed. Forges will primarily be used for working hot metal. The anvil must be fixed to a secure, sturdy base and positioned as close as possible to both the forge and the quenching tank.

Do not allow spilt fuel to lie on the floor. Always use gas ignition processes for the forge and wear safety boots and a leather apron at all times. Forges emit noxious fumes, so extraction is important. The flue should be designed so that all fumes are completely discharged into the outside atmosphere. **The area surrounding the forge should be constructed entirely of non-flammable materials. Keep all tools in a rack within easy reach of the working area.**

## Welding

Many of the hazards associated with welding have already been discussed. Fumes and gases are a cause of danger and they must not be inhaled. Avoid welding coated or galvanised metals – the fumes and gases produced by these are almost always difficult to predict accurately and are often extremely dangerous. Welding creates infra-red and ultraviolet radiation;

the former can cause burns, headaches, fatigue and eye damage, and the latter can cause extreme sunburn and skin tumours. It is obviously important to wear the correct protective clothing and face and eye masks.

Keep work clothes clean; oily, greasy clothing can be flammable. Do not use flammable materials such as turpentine in the vicinity of welding.

Electric arc welding brings the added hazard of electrocution. The currents are often well above the average, and can cause secondary electrical and mechanical hazards such as a shock making someone fall from a height. All equipment must be fully earthed. There should be an insulated hood to accommodate the electrode holder if it is not fully insulated.

**Do not weld on an asbestos cement or concrete base as both these materials can explode when heated – firebricks or a similar refractory material should be used.**

It is extremely important to ensure that no vessel being soldered, brazed or welded has contained a flammable liquid, as with, for example, the petrol tank of a car; in such cases, an explosion could occur. Vessels of this sort must be properly cleaned before work commences – see the Department of Employment's Health and Safety at Work booklet number 32: *Repair of Drums and Small Tanks: Explosion and Fire Risks.*

## Soldering

Be careful not to inhale the fumes from molten solder as these can contain lead. Zinc chloride fluxes are both toxic and corrosive, and you must wear barrier creams when handling them. Protective gloves are not as good because they are harder to clean once contaminated. Do not use solvents to clean zinc chloride fluxes from the skin – use special hand cleansers instead. Rosin (resin) fluxes may contain solvents and must be treated as a possible fire hazard.

Brazing (or hard soldering) involves higher temperatures than electrical or soft soldering. Some silver solders release toxic fumes. Fluoride fluxes which are used with silver solders can themselves release harmful fumes.

## Casting

Metal casting is becoming more and more popular with artists and craftspeople both as a leisure activity and a source of income. Hazards include the production of fumes, and the risk of burns, fire and explosion.

**All metal fumes can cause metal fume fever, a condition with symptoms similar to influenza. Zinc oxide fumes are especially likely to cause this.**

Molten brass, pewter and bronze release lead fumes. Casting often also produces carbon monoxide and silica dust; the former from incomplete combustion of fuels or the burning of organic matter in moulding sand, and the latter from sand used in the shell moulding process. When shell moulding it is always better to use a micro-crystalline moulding compound rather than vinamould resin binders, which can release formaldehyde (formalin) and phenolic or ammonium vapours on decomposition.

The lost wax process, in which a wax shape is melted out of the mould, presents its own hazards. Silica, solvents and acids are all present in the fire-resistant plaster used as a negative mould. One form of the process uses styrofoam or polyurethane foam to make the positive moulds – these release toxic fumes on burning.

## Surface finishing

Chemical finishing of metals includes anodising, chromium plating and electroplating. With anodising, use sulphuric rather than chromic acid, which will minimise the risks, providing that adequate ventilation is ensured.

Chromium plating can be extremely dangerous and must be completely segregated from all other processes. Reference should be made to the 'Chromium Plating Regulations 1931 and 1973' for detailed advice. Although these are intended for industrial users they offer detailed rules of great importance to anybody embarking on such activities.

Electroplating involves the use of cyanide. This must never come into contact with acids, as hydrogen cyanide vapours will be produced. Hydrogen cyanide is extremely poisonous and will cause serious illness and, rapidly, death.

Mechanical finishing is usually achieved by grinding and abrasing. The only serious hazards are air-borne dusts, for which suitable protective clothing should be worn, and the risk of clothes catching in machinery.

## Metalworking machinery and tools

Metalworking machinery must follow the rules of safe guarding which were outlined earlier in the book. Whilst metalworking machines tend to run slower than their woodworking counterparts, they are very powerful. Guards must be used at all times and loose hair and clothing must be kept tied back.

**Eye protection is important; metalwork processes often create sparks and splinters of metal. Wear eye-cup goggles or safety glasses with side shields.**

Metalworking machines tend to be heavy and expensive, and consequently are not used by the home craftsperson as often as are woodworking machines. If you do buy a machine such as a lathe or pillar drill, it is essential to contact the manufacturer for advice on siting, or to follow any instructions provided. Various factors such as the preparation of the floor, correct maintenance and power supply will have to be considered before the machine can be operated properly.

Metalworking guillotines must be properly guarded to limit access to the blade from any angle. When they are not in use they must be secured either by removing the handle or by using a locking mechanism.

Metalworking tools and machine bits, like any other cutting edges, must be kept well sharpened and well maintained. Be particularly careful with the striking end of cutting tools such as cold chisels or brick bolsters where the power is supplied with a hammer blow. After continuous use, the hammer flattens out the top forming a 'mushroom' of metal splinters. These can be thrown up into the eye and should be filed down carefully and regularly.

# Motor maintenance

With the escalating costs of service and parts, repairing and maintaining cars has become an essential skill for many people. Whether you are changing a wheel by the roadside or removing an engine in a garage, motor maintenance can present serious and often potentially-fatal risks.

It is beyond the scope of this book to examine every risk in every process involved in maintaining your car. Before embarking on anything other than the simplest of tasks, it is essential that you obtain an authoritative manual or handbook. Instruction manuals supplied with the vehicle are rarely adequate; whilst they may describe the components of the car in detail, they are unlikely to give comprehensive advice on removing, handling or replacing them. There are a number of popular 'owners' manuals available in bookshops. Buy the book that covers both your make and model of car and follow its instructions exactly.

Remember that your work may affect the proper performance of the vehicle and that the vehicle's performance may affect the safety of other drivers and road users, or of pedestrians. If you are in doubt about anything, it is essential that you seek professional advice.

Keep children and pets away from the work area and do not let them play in or around the vehicle, especially when it is unattended. If you are doing work that involves jacking up the vehicle or lifting heavy weights (such as the engine – see p.158), let someone know and ask them to check on you occasionally.

Before starting the engine, double-check that the gear (or transmission) is in neutral or 'park' and that the hand-brake is on. If there is an incline and you are working underneath the car, use bricks as chocks behind the wheels to supplement the hand-brake, but remember to remove them before driving away.

## Hygiene

The importance of good housekeeping and hygiene has been

discussed elsewhere. Particular concerns in the garage include protection against personal contamination, and spills of liquids such as oil and grease, which must be cleaned up immediately with a suitable solvent.

Oil can cause a number of skin complaints, so wear a good barrier cream or gloves whilst you are working. Avoid untidy or cluttered work areas. Remember to protect your eyes with impact-resistant glasses or goggles where necessary, especially if you are working on your back underneath the vehicle.

Always work in a logical and methodical manner – this will make things easier as well as safer.

## Mechanical safety

Always be careful when you inspect or repair a running engine. Keep long hair, ties, scarves or shirt cuffs away from moving parts.

If you are jacking the vehicle up, use a supplementary form of support such as axle stands or even piles of bricks. Place these under a part of the car or chassis that you are certain will not fail. Jack the car up higher than the supplementary supports and lower it on to them once they are in place; this will ensure that they are all supporting the vehicle together. This precaution is essential when you have to work under the vehicle.

When changing a wheel, do not attempt to tighten (or loosen) 'high-torque' nuts whilst the vehicle is jacked up off the ground as this may pull the car off the jack. High-torque nuts, such as those on a wheel hub, require considerable turning power when they are being removed or fitted. Instead, loosen the nuts whilst the car is still on the ground and then remove them once it has been jacked up. When replacing the wheel, half-tighten the nuts whilst the vehicle is off the ground and fully-tighten them once you have jacked it down to a position either on or just off the ground. Avoid jacking up vehicles that are on an incline.

If you are unsure of your ability to lift a weight, either get assistance or buy, borrow or rent some form of lifting tackle (such as a 'block and tackle'). If you use a lifting tackle ensure that it is more than capable of handling the load you want it to move.

Always try to match nuts or bolts with a tool of the correct size. Do not use ill-fitting spanners or wrenches that could slip and injure you.

**Many engine parts become hot whilst they are functioning. Never drain oil before it has had time to cool. Boiling, or even hot, oil can cause very serious burns and scalds.**

So be careful when grasping or touching any part of the engine or exhaust systems after the vehicle has been running; always check gingerly to see whether they are hot. Do not suddenly remove the cap from radiators or cooling systems as steam or hot coolants may escape and scald you. If there is a pressure release valve use it, and put a cloth or a wet rag over the cap before slowly undoing it. Wait until the pressure has gone before removing the cap.

## Electrical safety

Some of the voltages you might encounter are quite high and must be treated with caution. The ignition system in particular must not be touched whilst the engine is running or being cranked. In cars with an electronic ignition system the voltages are much higher and could even prove fatal.

Never work on the electrical system without first removing the battery earth terminal (or the 'ground' terminal).

Be careful when 'jump starting' a vehicle. If you use a booster battery for negative earth (or ground) vehicles, connect the positive leads first and then connect the negative of the booster battery to an earthing point on the car you wish to start. Make sure that the earthing point is at least two feet from the battery if possible. Do not touch any moving parts and make sure that the vehicles are not touching.

Do not confuse the negative terminal of a car battery with the neutral terminal of a domestic circuit; electrical systems in cars are direct current (dc).

## Fire safety

Fire hazards include petroleum, or petroleum distillates, and hydrogen released from car batteries. Never smoke or use a naked flame whilst working on your car. Remember that sparks from short circuits or static electricity can ignite flammable vapours. Disconnect the earth terminal of the battery before any work involving the vehicle's fuel system.

**Never allow naked flames near the battery and do not cause sparks. Car batteries normally give off some hydrogen, which is a highly flammable gas.**

Buy a fire extinguisher to keep near the car whilst you are working on it. The best type will be a Halon (or BCF) type which comes either with a green label or in a green cylinder.

## Chemical safety

Potentially toxic liquids include petroleum, anti-freeze and brake fluids – do not syphon these using your mouth. Avoid breathing petroleum or solvent fumes, as these can quite quickly cause unconsciousness and even death if inhaled in sufficiently high concentrations.

Exhaust fumes contain carbon monoxide and, in the United Kingdom, lead; the former can prove fatal quickly, the latter can cause longer-term damage. Do not run the engine inside the garage and always avoid breathing the fumes.

With batteries, remember that the electrolyte is an acid and can be corrosive even when diluted. Be careful when topping the battery up and always add acid to water if mixing your own solution. If you add water to acid, droplets of water will turn to steam and cause the acid to spit out. Take all the usual precautions to protect yourself against the acid, including protective clothing.

Some parts of the car may contain asbestos. Many authorities believe that there is no safe level of exposure to asbestos, so the utmost care must be taken when handling such components. Those that may contain asbestos include friction, sealing and insulation parts such as brake linings, brake bands, clutch linings, torque convertors, gaskets and so on. Maintain a high level of hygiene when working with such parts and do not eat, drink or smoke in the vicinity of your activity. Even though the quantities of asbestos are small, it is essential to avoid breathing any dusts given off. Buy a suitable face mask and remember that the most dangerous fibres are the microscopic ones.

# Painting

## *Art and craft*

Materials encountered by the artist or craftsperson can be divided into two categories: pigments (colours) and solvents (see p.132).

Pigments are most dangerous when they are ground or mixed as a dust. At such times they can present a hazard by inhalation, ingestion or skin contact. When grinding or mixing large quantities of pigment, avoid spilling or disturbing the dust. If the atmosphere does become dusty, wear a suitable face mask.

Spraying paints with an aerosol, air brush or compressed air gun will leave a fine mist of pigment and solvent in the air. This mixture is flammable, so exposure to naked flames must be avoided. If the work is done for long periods of time or in appreciable quantities, wear a face mask and ensure adequate ventilation.

Skin contact with pigments should be avoided. Some, such as cobalt and chrome pigments, may irritate the skin, cause allergies and even be carcinogenic (cancer causing). Coal tar pigments are recognised carcinogens and may cause photosensitisation, a skin allergy to light. Absorption of pigments through the skin may be aided by solvents, either directly or through cuts or scratches.

Cinnobar and vermilion can contain mercuric sulphide, and burnt umber, raw umber, manganese brown and Mars brown can all contain manganese dioxide. Cerulean blue, cobalt blue and Thernards blue can contain cobalt oxide. Chromium green, green viridium and guignets green can all contain chromium. Cobalt green can contain cobalt oxide or zinc oxide. Emerald green, pear green and Scheeles green might contain traces of arsenic, as could cobalt violet. Manganese blue sometimes contains barium as well as manganese. The various whites between them could contain zinc oxide, lead carbonate, barium sulphate and titanium dioxide; yellows could contain barium chromate, lead chromate, zinc chromate, chromium, cadmium sulphate, cobalt, lead and antimony.

Whilst most of these chemicals are contained in small quantities only, they could still prove harmful. Avoid eating or drinking with paint-covered hands and wash working clothes regularly. Under no circumstances 'point' the tip of the brush with your mouth.

## Painting and decorating

Decorating paints also contain some dangerous chemicals, most notably lead. Some years ago most primers contained enough lead to cause harm if sufficient amounts were consumed. However, general awareness of the dangers of lead has eliminated the lead content of most paints, and reduced it in the rest. Nevertheless, it is important to check that primers do not contain lead, especially where children's toys are concerned. If you are painting things meant for children, such as toys, playpens, or highchairs, it is essential that the paints conform to the Toy Safety Regulations. If this is not clear on the can, contact the technical services department of the manufacturer and ask for clarification. Most child-safe paints will, however, state this fact quite clearly. Be especially careful with brightly coloured paints.

**If you are priming galvanised metal, you will almost certainly have to use a lead-based paint; calcium plumbate primer seems to be the only one suitable. In such a case, the rules of good hygiene are of paramount importance – wash hands regularly, avoid eating or drinking whilst working and avoid contamination of the living area.**

Do remember that, while modern paints are unlikely to contain lead or other harmful chemicals, old paint may do. If you are sanding or stripping old or brightly coloured paint, wear a dust mask with a suitably fine filter. Follow all the rules of good hygiene.

Be careful of paints that contain fungicides and try to avoid those that warn you to keep them away from children or pets – try to use a substitute, such as a paint that does not contain a fungicide at all!

If you are using a solvent-based paint, ensure adequate ventilation to clear the fumes. Remember that fumes or chemicals too weak to harm you may hurt or even kill pets. Typical of this would be tropical fish or goldfish kept in aquaria – such animals can be extremely sensitive to chemical pollution of their water.

## Blowlamps and paint strippers

There are two main methods of stripping old paint, both of which can be dangerous.

Blowlamps tend to be fuelled by either gas or paraffin. Paraffin blowlamps are cheap to run, but they create a lot of mess and can be both difficult and sometimes dangerous to light. Gas blowlamps will function either off a small cylinder or canister underneath the torch, or off a separate cylinder connected by a pipe.

**Always place a non-flammable sheet underneath the area you will be stripping – a cheap fire blanket is ideal for this purpose. Do not place newspaper to catch the scrapings as these are often still alight as they fall.**

Keep a small fire extinguisher, plant-spray or washing-up liquid bottle full of water close at hand whilst working. Find a non-flammable surface such as a metal tray, ceramic tile or large, level fire brick to stand the blowlamp on if you need to put it down while working. Always be careful when scraping the burnt paint off the surface. If you point the blowlamp away from the wall while scraping, check that it does not point at anything that could burn and that it is not in such a position that anybody could walk into its flame. Always wear non-flammable gloves. Hot paint scrapings are capable of inflicting painful burns – avoid plastic or rubber gloves, which could melt into the skin.

Chemical paint strippers are popular for their versatility,

and for their safety on flammable surfaces or on fragile surfaces, such as glass, where a blowlamp would be quite unsuitable. Chemical paint strippers can be messy and dangerous and must be used with caution. The most common strippers are solvent-based and contain dichloromethane. Others are caustic and contain caustic soda (sodium hydroxide).

**All paint strippers can burn or irritate the skin, so protective clothing must be worn, including rubber or plastic gloves, goggles and old clothes. Any splashes must be washed from the skin immediately with water.**

Cover furniture or floors with sheets of polythene and collect scrapings in a metal box, bin or tin. Try to avoid leaving scrapings lying on the floor. If you are using caustic strippers, which are supplied either in a ready-to-use paste or as pellets that must be dissolved in water, you may find that they darken the natural colour of the wood. If you want to retain the natural finish, it might be necessary to use bleach to correct any discolouring; follow the manufacturer's instructions precisely, avoid skin or eye contact and remove the bleach with plenty of water afterwards.

# Photography

Electrical safety in the darkroom has already been examined in the section on electrical hazards in the bathroom. Most of the remaining hazards relate to the chemicals used and to their proper handling.

## Chemical safety

Mixing stock solutions from dry powders is the most prominent hazard as the chemicals are in their most concentrated form. It is important to wear the correct protective clothing when doing this, or when putting prints into solutions. A lab coat and face mask must be worn whilst mixing stock solutions; the face mask is essential as the base chemicals are in powder form and can be inhaled. Rubber or plastic gloves are always useful and those that come in bulk are ideal. Do not, however, use barrier creams; there is some evidence that they can combine with photographic chemicals and increase the risk of skin irritation.

Both the darkroom and any other room used to mix photographic chemicals must be kept well ventilated. It is a good idea to have a proper extractor fan fitted; a minimum strength of twelve air changes per hour is a good working standard.

## Hygiene

Cleanliness is of the utmost importance. Spillages of any liquid or powder must be cleaned up instantly and all working surfaces kept clear. Cover all benches or tables with a non-absorbent material such as formica. Keep all photographic chemicals sealed in their correct bottles and well out of the reach of children. Wherever possible, use tongs or paddles to put prints in or out of solution.

Most photographic chemicals are not flammable, so fire hazards are limited. Do not, however, smoke in the darkroom and label any flammable chemicals that you use there.

Paradoxical though it may seem, you should always ensure good levels of lighting in the darkroom, both with the main light and in particular with the safe lights. Position these over the work areas; one over the enlarger and one over the developer, stop and fix (or hypam) trays would be sufficient though three or more lights might be necessary over a large or cluttered work area.

It is important that skin contact with chemicals is avoided. Although they are not all dermatitic they may cause skin sensitisation over long periods of time.

**People who suffer from any type of skin disease or from allergies such as hay fever or asthma must be especially careful – experience suggests that their skin tends to be more sensitive.**

When mixing chemicals, follow the manufacturer's instructions precisely. Chemicals supplied by reputable companies always contain instruction leaflets and sticky-back labels to put on to the stock solution containers – use these.

If you are using photographic chemicals on a regular basis, it might be wise to consult your GP or have a medical examination. Particular concerns here are allergies, colour blindness or sensitivity to particular chemicals.

Wash any chemical splashes off the skin with plenty of water no matter what the chemical may be.

Be particularly careful when branching out into colour developing; there is some evidence that colour developers are more likely to cause irritations or problems than black and white ones.

Eyes must also be protected. If eyes are splashed at all, wash them with water for ten to fifteen minutes. If they feel irritated for any period of time afterwards, take medical advice. You may feel it is a good idea to buy an industrial eye wash station to put on to the wall of your darkroom. These are not expensive for the smaller units and contain one or two bottles of distilled water that can be pressed over the eye to flush out any chemicals that have entered it.

If you do have an established allergy to a specific chemical, the list below should adequately cover all those contained in photographic products. However, manufacturers of photographic chemicals tend to be co-operative when presented with any enquiry regarding health, so do not hesitate to contact them if you feel that you need further advice.

Developers may contain acetic acid, benzyl alcohol, boric acid (borax), ethylene diamine, ethyl glycol, glutaraldehyde, hydroquinine, potassium hydroxide, pyrocatechin, pyrogallic acid and sodium hydroxide.

Stop baths are almost invariably acetic acid, but as their only purpose is to neutralise the alkalinity of the developer, other mild acids are sometimes used. Be careful not to inhale the fumes from bottles of the concentrated acid – they are very powerful indeed.

Fixing (or hypam) solutions might contain ammonium chloride, boric acid or potassium chrome alum. Old solutions will also contain quantities of silver or its compounds.

Bleachers, reducers or dye bleachers in their various forms could contain ammonia, formaldehyde (or formalin), hydrochloric acid, hydrogen peroxide, perchloric acid, potassium bromide, potassium cyanide, potassium ferricyanide, sulphuric acid or thiocarbonide.

Intensifiers contain hydrochloric acid, lead acetate, potassium dichromate, potassium ferricyanide, pyrocatechin, pyrogallic acid, and sodium hydroxide.

Toning includes the use of potassium bromide, sodium sulphide, sulphuric acid and thiocarbamide.

Other chemicals with which you might come into contact include acetone, calcium chloride, carbolic acid, glycerin, oxalic acid, silver nitrate and vanadium chloride.

# Printing

You only need to examine a 'fly-posting' wall in any city centre to see how many people make use of printing. In addition to pop groups, local campaign organisers and organisers of jumble sales, almost every branch of every major political party has access to some form of amateur printing system. Two forms are likely to be used: silkscreen and lithography.

## *Silkscreen*

Silkscreen inks and colours use the same pigments as oil paints (see p.161) and the same precautions should be taken. Beyond these the main hazards are presented by the solvents used in inks, bases, thinners, retarders and general wash fluids. Inks may be anything up to 70 per cent solvent, bases 80 per cent, and thinners and retarders 100 per cent, so the rules for handling and using solvents must be observed carefully. Avoid leaving cans of ink open, or large quantities of ink on a palette for any time, as solvent vapours will be constantly evaporating into the atmosphere. Ventilation is important. If possible, exhaust fans should be fitted. A local, high-velocity exhaust duct is the most economical and effective device, but this is unlikely to prove feasible for most people.

After cleaning up work areas, all unused inks, solvents or

rags should either be disposed of or securely bottled and stored. Put rags in a sealed bin outside, or dispose of them by controlled burning.

Do not let the screen dry to such an extent that an excess of clean-up solvent has to be used. If you decide to use acetone as a substitute cleaning solvent, bear in mind that it presents a considerable fire hazard.

In the process of photo-screen printing a light-sensitive emulsion containing highly-toxic potassium dichromate and ammonium dichromate is sometimes used. Be very careful with these chemicals.

Other dangerous chemicals likely to be encountered include: alkyd resins (which release toxic gases like carbon monoxide, formaldehyde and acrolein), aromatic and aliphatic hydrocarbons, butyl acetate, butyl cellulose, cellulose acetate, denatured ethanol, diacetone alcohol, ethyl acetate, hydrogen peroxide, isopropanol, isophorone, methanol, methylene chloride, methyl cellulose, mineral spirits, napthenes, olefins, paraffins, resins, trichlorethylene ('Supaklene') and xylene. Most of these are solvents.

Silkscreen equipment is fairly harmless, with the exception of process camera lamps. These operate at a power of 3,000 watts and generate a great deal of heat. Do not touch the bulbs even when they are cold, as this can cause them to shatter once they are in use. Be careful with mercury vapour lamps in printing-down tables for these can cause skin burns and eye problems such as conjunctivitis.

## Lithography

As with all printing processes, try to use ready-made products in preference to mixing your own. This minimises contact with harmful chemicals. Various desensitising etches contain potassium dichromate, nitric acid and phosphoric acid. All of these are extremely dangerous and must therefore be handled with care.

Lithographic crayons and tushe contain lamp black, a suspected carcinogen that can cause irritation. Avoid any contact with the skin.

Some of the talcum powders in talc/resin mixes contain

asbestos, which can cause asbestosis, lung cancer and a rare cancer known as 'mesothelioma'. Use asbestos-free talcs such as cosmetic or baby powder instead.

Other dangerous chemicals which might be used include acetic acid, alcohols, ammonium nitrate, aromatic nitrates, aromatic and aliphatic hydrocarbons, carbolic acid, carboxyl methyl, cellulose, cellusolve acetate, chrome alum, di-acetone alcohol, di-isobutyl ketone, epoxy resins, ethyl acetate, ethylene glycol, hydrofluoric acid, isopropyl alcohol, isopropane, methanol, methyl cellulose, methylene chloride, monomethyl ether, acetone, phosphoric acid, sodium dichromate, toluene, xylene, zinc chloride and zinc nitrate.

Check the label of any product used to see whether it contains any of these chemicals; if necessary, contact the manufacturer for further information.

# Woodwork

Working with wood is probably everybody's image of the typical DIY activity – and with some justification. The ease with which the raw materials can be obtained, and the training that most children (girls as well as boys) get at school, makes carpentry the ideal way of elaborating, expanding and repairing one's environment.

Although hand tools such as chisels, saws and hammers, pose some obvious hazards, it is the machines that cause the greatest danger. They will be specifically examined in this section, but the general rules of operational and electrical safety discussed earlier for DIY machine and power tools apply in full.

Woodworking machines are more dangerous than their metalworking counterparts, primarily because of their tremendous operating speeds – metalworking machines are slow in comparison.

Do not buy bench-mounted machines without taking professional advice on their safe usage. Your local education authority will probably provide woodworking lessons in the evenings at a sufficiently advanced level, or be able to advise you of suitable alternative local training bodies.

## Bandsaw

Release the blade tension when the machine is not in use. Only make adjustments when the machine is switched off, and keep the guard down at all times. Correctly patterned blades should be kept well sharpened and should not be distorted. Only apply brakes when absolutely necessary. The teeth of the saw blade must be sufficiently set so as not to cause kick back of the timber being cut.

## Circular saw

The saw blade must be fully guarded at all times, even when the machine is not in use. Beware of old machines bought from lumber yards or timber merchants – these are often extremely badly guarded. If the machine is a bench saw, check underneath that the lower half of the blade is guarded – children and pets run a terrible risk if they crawl underneath.

The teeth of the blade must be sharp, and must be correctly set, tensioned and profiled to ensure that kick back of the timber is avoided.

## Planing machine

Guards should always be used with scrupulous care. Ensure that the table, knives and fence are all secured carefully. With thicknessers, be careful working on old floor boards or doors. Remove all nails, bolts or fittings, and check that no nail or screw bodies are hidden below the surface.

## Vertical spindle moulding machines

**These are perhaps the most dangerous of all woodworking machines. They must only be used with great caution and by following the manufacturer's instructions precisely.**

Injuries to the hand, including severed fingers, are the most common injuries, and result from carelessness and ignorance of the correct way to use and adjust guards as often as from failure to fix guards altogether. Trial cutting before commencing the major work is the time when most people seem to 'skip' the inconvenience of using the guards – never do this. It cannot be over-emphasised that the guards on a vertical spindle moulding machine must be used and properly adjusted whenever the machine is running.

Always be alert when cutting wood – variations in grain, texture, twists and knots can all cause the wood to jump. Wherever possible, use implements such as jigs, push-sticks and holders, and always keep hands well away from the cutting edge.

Blunt tools are dangerous, and must never be used. This is true of all woodworking machines and tools, but especially so of vertical spindle moulders. Take the trouble of checking the edge and of grinding and sharpening blunt tools. Most DIY shops will be able to do this for you.

Similar precautions should be taken for routers as for spindle moulding machines.

## Chemical hazards

Some wood dusts can cause respiratory problems and dermatitis, and all cause fire hazards of varying severity. Be particularly careful with South American boxwood, western red cedar, cocobolo, ebony, greenheart, ipe, iroko, American and African mahogany, makone, mansenia, obeche, opepe, red and white peroba, East Indian and Brazilian rosewood, satinwood, teak and wenge. All these can damage the respiratory system and cause skin and eye allergies, and some are suspected of causing nasal cancer.

In addition, arbor vitæ, beech, birch, cocopod, dahoma, dogwood, guarea, katon, maple, myrtle, pine, redwood, sequoia redwood, slavewood, and sneeze wood can cause respiratory problems, and ayan, African blackwood, cashew, cocus, ramin and sucupia may cause skin or eye allergies.

Generally, respiratory ailments occur as the result of long periods of exposure to the dust, but some types of dust can cause problems in a few hours, depending on the level and circumstances of exposure, and the individual. Long-term exposure can produce 'fogged' lungs on X-rays, and a type of occupational asthma that in some cases becomes practically permanent.

171

Local exhaust extraction is the best way to keep the dust levels down. In essence, this will mean extraction methods that capture the dust while it is still in the machine. Many dust-producing DIY machines come with filters and dust bags, or can be fitted with them at little extra cost.

**Local exhaust is essential for planing machines used for thicknessing wood, multi-cutter moulding machines, automatic lathes, high-speed routers and tensioning machines.**

If atmospheric dust does become a problem, suitable goggles and a face mask must be worn. Try to clean up fine dust with wet cleaning methods wherever possible, even if this means spraying it with water. Dry brushing will just stir dust up into the air again.

Anybody prone to skin complaints such as dermatitis should seriously consider protecting themselves with suitable clothing and barrier creams – dust, oil, sap and wood extracts from many species can cause irritations and allergies.

When you buy wood from your local DIY centre or timber merchant remember that it may have been treated with pesticides or preservatives. Chipboard, blockboard and plywood are treated with phenolic and amino resins, which can be harmful. Be careful when machining these timbers and avoid inhaling any dust. Other hazardous chemicals that may be encountered include cresylic acid, copper hydrate, ethyl triethanol amine, napthenic acid, pentachlorophenol and potassium dichromate.

Woodworkers whose activities consume long and regular periods of their time should guard their health carefully. Treat any health problem which improves after a few days lay off, and which returns when work is resumed, as possibly related to woodworking.

Where exposure to wood dusts is considerable, ask your doctor to arrange a pulmonary function test every two or three years. Such a test can detect lung problems much sooner than an X-ray.

# FIRST AID

## What is first aid?

First aid, or immediate care, actually covers quite a wide range of different functions. Indeed, it covers as many functions as people suffer injuries. For most of us, our knowledge of first aid will thankfully only be drawn upon for minor ailments such as cuts, bruises, insect stings and so on. But in some cases, a thorough knowledge of first aid can make the difference between a comparatively controllable injury, and a tragedy. For example, if the victim of a minor accident unexpectedly stops breathing, artificial resuscitation, applied in the correct way until an ambulance arrives, could well save their life.

Equally, minor cuts and bruises that do not require medical attention can be more successfully treated if you have a sound knowledge of first aid. A small cut that is improperly cleaned and dressed may become infected; simple first aid practised properly can significantly reduce the chances of that happening.

The knowledge that you can acquire from books such as this and, more importantly, from the first aid training courses offered by recognised bodies, will remove the feeling of helplessness that often paralyses us when we witness a serious accident. The rules of first aid will enable you to take charge of the casualty's welfare until professional aid can arrive. The rules of first aid will thus enable you to help the doctors, nurses and ambulancemen in their jobs. This is because the first few seconds or minutes after an injury are critical. Minimising blood loss, reassuring the casualty and making them comfortable, and collecting information for the doctors to use once the casualty arrives at hospital will all contribute to the future well-being of the casualty.

This largely answers the question 'What is first aid?'. There are, of course, many things to learn to be fully prepared. How you apply artificial resuscitation or heart compression; how you stop bleeding; how you treat burns or scalds. The list may appear endless, but the essence of first aid is the willingness to prepare yourself to help your fellow men and women if they need you.

Only one real note of caution is needed here. We hope that the following guide to simple first aid will help you to help others, and that it may encourage you to seek proper training from an organisation such as the St. John Ambulance Brigade, your local authority, or any of the other bodies listed at the end of this book. But it is often said that a little knowledge can be more dangerous than none at all and this is certainly true of first aid. 'Having a go' is not a good policy and first aiders must recognise that they are not doctors. If there is ever any doubt about the nature or extent of an injury then you must seek professional help. The role of the first aider is to support, not supplant the full-time medical services. We hope the information in this book will help you to do that.

# Basics first

## *First-aid kits*

Most people thinking of first aid immediately think of a first-aid box or kit and it is certainly true that every home should have one. You can either buy a made-up kit, or buy the individual components to make one up yourself. In either case, the kit should be kept in one place, preferably in a tailor-made enamelled or plastic box. This is partly for reasons of portability, but also for reasons of hygiene as they are designed to be easily cleaned. You should wash your cabinet regularly with a mild antiseptic solution to prevent dirt or germs from collecting.

Your box should not have a lock, nor should it contain any medicines. Medicines, including analgesics (pain killers such as aspirin and paracetamol) should be kept in a separate, locked medicine cabinet. Keep your first-aid box out of the reach of children but make sure that everybody knows where it is.

Contents should include: cotton wool, a range of small, medium and large sterilised unmedicated dressings, assorted sizes of sticking-plasters, bandages (1, 1½ and 2 inches wide), a roll of sticking-plaster at least 1 inch wide, an assortment of safety pins, a thermometer, a small pair of scissors, and an antiseptic such as Dettol or TCP.

Other items you may wish to add include a small eye wash, a pair of tweezers for splinters and some antiseptic ointment. Buy your first aid supplies from reputable chemists or dealers and replace them whenever necessary. For instance, if your tweezers start to rust replace them immediately with a new pair.

Also remember to take your cabinet on holiday with you. For day trips and picnics, you may find it easier to buy a small, portable kit in a plastic or metal box. Make sure that your first-aid box does not become a general bathroom cabinet; nailclippers, toothpaste and mouthwash will all start to occupy a permanent place in your cabinet if you do not take care!

## What to do in an emergency

An emergency requiring first aid could be either an injury, or a sudden illness such as a heart attack. In either case, you must use your knowledge to take control in a calm but firm manner. If somebody else present has a better knowledge of immediate care than you, then you must support them in any way possible. If you are the most able person present then it will be your responsibility to control the course of events.

STEP ONE is always to call for PROFESSIONAL HELP. If it is possible, then send a bystander to call for an ambulance and, if you feel the situation requires it, the police as well. You must make sure that the person who is sent for help understands the basic information which they must pass on, including the cause and location of the accident, the number and age of the injured, and the severity of the injuries. The information will be invaluable to the hospital. If they know, for instance, that the accident was a car crash and one of the victims is unconscious and suffering from severe head injuries, they can prepare themselves for an emergency.

STEP TWO is to MINIMISE ANY DANGER to either yourself or the casualty. In the event of a road accident somebody must ensure that there is no danger posed by the traffic until a policeman arrives. Likewise, where a casualty has been electrocuted, it is necessary to ensure that they are not in contact with the current before you touch them. If they are, then you must break the contact either at source or at the casualty (see p.190).

In general, minimising danger is a matter for common sense. If somebody is lying unconscious in a room filled with gas, it is obviously necessary to switch off the gas, open the windows and if possible remove the casualty into the open air before commencing first aid. The same is true of casualties trapped under weights or by fire – release them from the immediate cause of injury before beginning first aid.

STEP THREE is to ASSESS the nature of the injuries and decide whether or not you should apply first aid. Here the untrained first aider is at a disadvantage. Before any form of treatment is given it is necessary to be sure that you are not going to compound another injury. For instance, if the casualty is unconscious, then the trained first aider would place them into the 'recovery position'. This is a position that would allow ease of breathing and recovery whilst preventing the casualty from choking on their own blood or vomit. But if that casualty also had a broken back, moving them into the recovery position might compound their injury. A trained first aider can decide about this because they know the correct way to check the nature and extent of many internal injuries. Once again, this illustrates the value of taking a proper first-aid training course if possible.

There are, however, a number of immediate and self-evident injuries that the untrained first aider can alleviate. These are listed below with their appropriate responses. Under each category there is a passage explaining the effects of different types of injury or illness and the symptoms that you should watch out for. This is followed by a short list of suitable

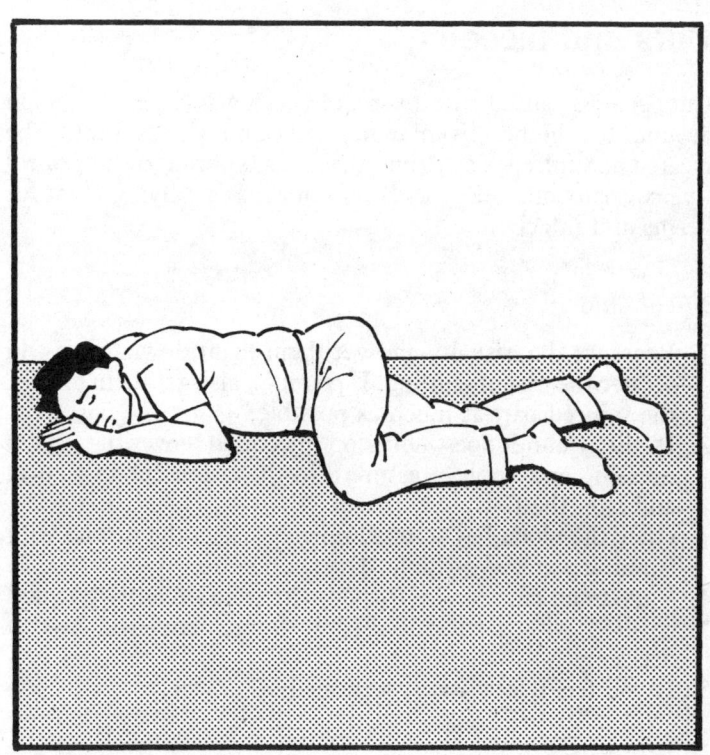

The recovery position

steps to take, but the general principles outlined above always apply and should always be followed.

Throughout the various sections reference will be made to reassuring the casualty. The importance of human warmth when dealing with an injured person cannot be over-emphasised. A casualty will often be shocked and frightened by the thought that their injuries are worse than they really are, or by the thought that they might even die. You must reassure them with optimistic and chatty talk while you are with them.

# Cuts and bleeding

Cuts can be caused by all sorts of accidents and are common around the home. Even minor cuts and grazes should be treated carefully, as anything that breaks through the protective covering offered by the skin can act as a rallying point for germs and infection.

## Small cuts

1. Reassure the casualty and get them to sit down. This will reduce the risk of fainting. If possible, also get them to raise the injured part as much as possible.
2. If the wound does not stop bleeding, cover it with a dressing and apply pressure directly to the cut to control and stop the flow.
3. Once the blood has stopped flowing, clean the wound with running water if possible. Dry with cotton wool.
4. Very small cuts can be treated with a liquid antiseptic and covered with a sticking-plaster. Larger cuts will need a dressing.
5. If you feel it necessary, seek medical advice.

## Serious cuts or bleeding

Serious cuts or bleeding can be extremely disturbing for both the casualty and the first aider. With serious bleeding, you must act quickly. The average adult has only about ten pints of blood and this can be lost in dangerous amounts quickly if a major artery or vein is severed. Your job is to stop or control the bleeding until medical help arrives.

1. Summon medical help. With a serious cut, do not hesitate to call 999 for an ambulance.
2. Apply pressure directly to the cut with your fingers. Do this with a dressing if possible. If the cut is large, pinch the sides together with your fingers. Under no circumstances apply a tourniquet as this can cause gangrene. Pressure should be maintained for at least five minutes, and may have to be continued for a long as fifteen minutes.

3. Ask the casualty to lie down and to raise the wounded part if possible. Also try to lower the casualty's head or raise their legs. Do not attempt to raise the injured area if you suspect that the casualty may have broken a bone.
4. If you do have a dressing, apply one to the wound and continue to apply new ones on top of the original one as necessary.
5. If a foreign body too big to be removed is still in the wound, apply pressure down its sides, or try to pinch the edges of the cut together as much as possible. If you can see particles or splinters in the cut which could easily be removed, then pick them out or wipe them out before continuing pressure.

## Internal bleeding

Many things can cause people to bleed internally, including a fracture, a severe bruise or fall, or various medical conditions. In some cases, such as a fractured skull or bleeding from internal organs, the bleeding may remain completely hidden. In others it may appear as bleeding from the ears or nose, as a blood-shot eye, as blood from the lungs, in vomit or excreta, or in urine. In all cases you must call emergency help. You should also do the following:
1. Lie the casualty down and raise their legs.
2. Loosen all tight clothing, and reassure the casualty.
3. Wrap the casualty up warmly.
Do not offer the casualty anything to eat or drink.

Some specific areas of bleeding require a slightly different approach. Common amongst these are cuts to the palm of the hand which can often bleed profusely. With these, cover the cut or cuts with a dressing followed by a pad or roll of bandage. When the fist is clenched it will then apply its own pressure to the wound.

Bleeding from extremely serious injuries such as a fractured skull, or chest or abdominal wounds should only be covered with dressings, and no pressure should be applied. In all such cases, priority should be given to getting the casualty to hospital as soon as possible. Try to place the casualty in a position of rest and loosen their clothing.

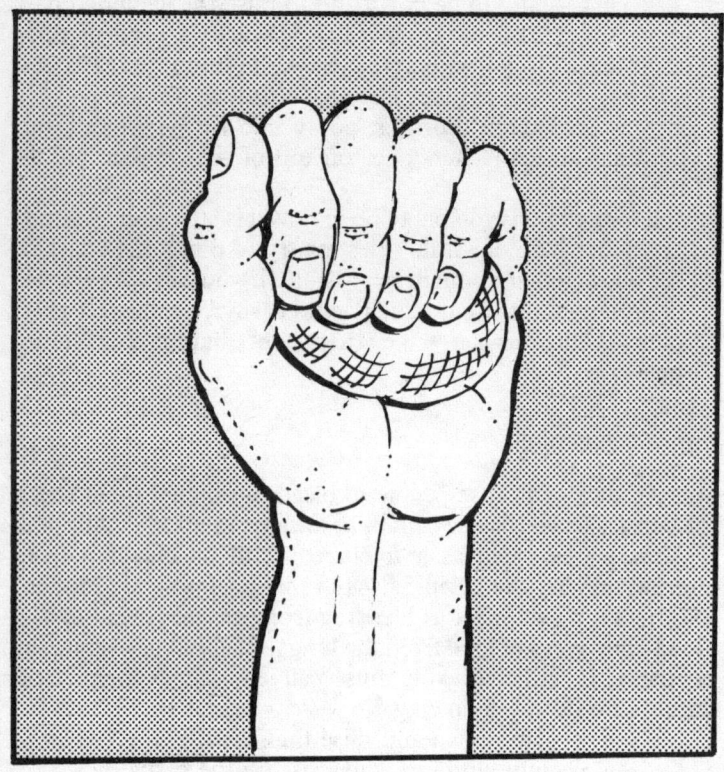

Treatment for a cut to the palm of the hand

## Choking and breathing problems

Choking or breathing problems are dangerous because they can prevent the body from receiving the oxygen it needs to survive. This condition, known as asphyxia, can cause breathing to become difficult and noisy, cause the lips, face, and finger and toe nails to turn blue, and may eventually cause a loss of consciousness.

Asphyxia may be caused by a number of things: food in the windpipe, suffocation with a pillow or plastic bag, strangulation, water or fluids in the windpipe, and so on. In all cases, you must act quickly and decisively.

## Choking

Although choking may not necessarily be caused by a blockage in the windpipe it can still cause muscular spasms that obstruct breathing. Irrespective of the age of the casualty, remove any obvious blockages from the mouth or throat. If you feel that there is a blockage in the windpipe, treatment is straightforward

If the casualty is a BABY:

1. Hold upside down by the legs.

Treatment for a choking baby (left) and child (right)

2. Smack the infant sharply on the back between the shoulder blades.
3. Repeat three or four times. This should dislodge any blockages.

If the casualty is a CHILD:
1. Lay over your knee with head pointing downwards.
2. Slap sharply between the shoulder blades three or four times to dislodge any blockages.

If the casualty is an ADULT:
1. Strike (rather than slap) three or four times between the shoulder blades to dislodge any blockages.

In all cases, if breathing difficulties continue, consult medical advice. If breathing stops or shows signs of stopping, apply artificial respiration (p.183).

## Strangulation or suffocation

Sadly, strangulation and hanging are common causes of both accidental and pre-meditated fatalities. They can be caused by a variety of things: by becoming caught in wires, ropes or cables, by allowing ties or clothing to become entangled in machinery, by assault or by attempted suicide. Suffocation can be caused, amongst other things, by polythene bags wrapped around the face, and by pillows.

In all cases, treatment is the same:
1. Release the casualty from the cause of injury. If this is a plastic bag, tear it open. If the casualty is hanging, lift them and loosen the cause of strangulation. If the casualty has an article of clothing caught in a machine, SWITCH OFF the machine instantly.
2. If breathing stops or shows signs of stopping, apply artificial respiration (see below) immediately.
3. Seek medical advice.

## Drowning

Speed is more important than ever when dealing with a drowning person. Do not waste time trying to expel water from their lungs; normally only a small amount will have entered them.

1. Remove any obstruction from the casualty's mouth.
2. Immediately commence artificial respiration (see below).
3. Arrange for emergency medical assistance.

# Artificial respiration and external heart compression

As the severity of an injury increases, the casualty will sometimes stop breathing. Shortly after this the heart will stop beating and within a few minutes they will die. On other occasions, such as during a heart attack, it may be the heart itself that fails first.

During the short time between respiratory or heart failure and death, the actions of any bystanders are critical. There are two mechanisms for sustaining life until emergency medical aid can arrive: artificial respiration and external heart compression. These are both best learned at organised classes where you can practise on life-size models with expert instruction, but the basic steps to follow are outlined below.

## *Artificial respiration*

(Mouth-to-mouth respiration, artificial resuscitation, kiss of life.) If the casualty's heart is still beating, but they have stopped breathing, you must act as their 'lungs' for them until they can either breathe for themselves, or until professional help arrives. This is to ensure that enough oxygen enters the lungs to sustain life. Although the air you provide will have already been in your lungs, most of it will still be oxygen.

1. Lay the casualty on their back with their head tilted back. Clear any obstructions from their mouth, but do not remove false teeth unless these have fallen out of place.
2. Pinch the casualty's nostrils tightly shut to prevent air escaping.
3. Open your mouth wide and take a deep breath of air.
4. Seal your lips tightly around the casualty's lips, holding their jaw open with your free hand.
5. Blow powerfully into the casualty's lungs until their chest rises up.

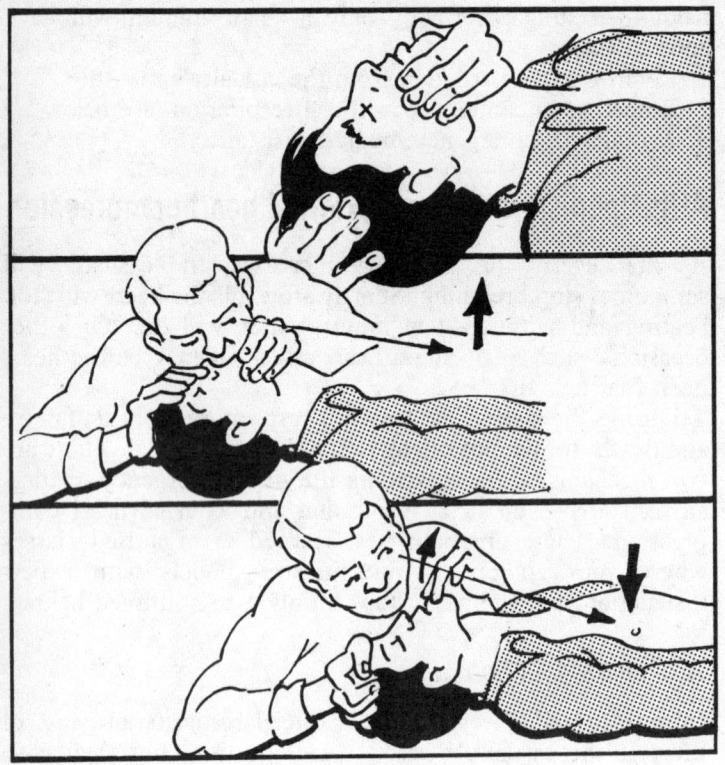

Artificial respiration

6. Remove your mouth and take another breath. Once the casualty's chest falls, repeat at the natural rate of breathing.

## External heart compression

If the casualty's heart has stopped beating, they will start to turn blue, most noticeably around the lips, and their pulse will have disappeared. This is because nothing is circulating the blood and its oxygen around the body. You will then have to fulfil the functions of both the breathing and the heart. The recommended way of doing this is: a) if you are by yourself, follow fifteen heart compressions (see below) with two lung inflations and repeat, and b) if you are with another first aider, follow five heart compressions with one lung inflation and repeat. One first aider should give the heart compressions and the other apply artificial respiration.

For an ADULT:

1. Kneel beside the casualty and feel their chest for the lower half of the breast bone.
2. Press the ball or heel of your palm against this, keeping the

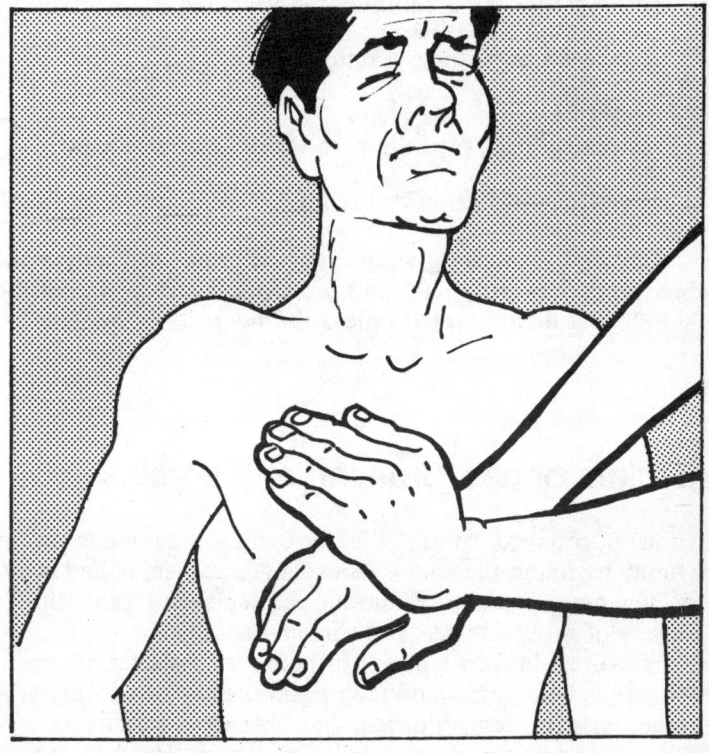

External heart compression

fingers and palm lifted off the bone. Cover this hand with the heel of the other hand so that the firmest parts of both palms (where they join the wrist) are pressing on the same spot.

3. Rock forward compressing the casualty's chest by pressing on the lower part of the breast bone. Keep both arms straight. The breast bone can be pushed in about one and a half inches.

4. Release the pressure, then repeat at least 60 times a minute.

For a CHILD:
1. As above, but light pressure with just one hand will be sufficient for children under ten years old.

2. Repeat 80 or 90 times a minute.

For a BABY:
1. Extremely light pressure with two fingers is sufficient.

2. Repeat about 100 times a minute.

**Artificial respiration should not be attempted unless the breathing has stopped, and external heart compression should not be attempted unless the heart has stopped.**


# Broken bones, bruising and sprains

Injuries received from falling are inevitably going to be common around the home. As explained earlier, falling is one of the most common domestic accidents and can cause a variety of broken bones, bruising and sprains.

Fractures (broken bones) can take two basic forms: open, where the bone sticks through the skin, and closed, where the fractured parts remain inside. In either case, serious damage can be done by any heavy-handed treatment. Because of this, your response must be limited.

Also because of this, treatment of severe bruises or sprains must be careful and cautious. It can be very difficult for the untrained first aider to tell if a fracture exists; you must always presume that such injuries might also include a fracture and seek medical advice.

In general, the following treatment should be given:

1. Avoid moving the casualty. Cover them with a blanket or coat to keep them warm and try to support the injured part if possible.
2. Cover any wound (i.e. with an open fracture) and try to control bleeding.
3. Summon medical help.
4. Avoid giving the casualty food or drink.

# Burns and scalds

Burns and scalds are a frequent cause of injury around the home and can often be very serious indeed. Even minor burns can prove serious where small children or babies are concerned, for whom medical attention should be sought without delay.

When treating burns, two factors should always be remembered. Firstly, the burn will in all probability still contain a great deal of heat. This will be injuring the casualty and causing them discomfort even though contact with the original heat source has been broken. Secondly, intense heat kills germs, so a burn will almost certainly be sterile. You must try to keep it that way whilst giving treatment.

Burns can be caused by a number of different sources, including: direct heat, such as a fire, the sun or hot objects; chemical heat, which might include acids and alkalis; friction; and electricity, which sometimes causes very deep burns.

A scald is essentially a type of burn and is caused generally by hot liquids such as steam, hot drinks, hot oil or hot tar. In both burns and scalds, symptoms include severe pain, redness and swelling, and shock. In all cases, the following steps should be taken:

1. Immerse the burnt part in water until pain stops. This is primarily to remove any heat in the burn, but in the case of chemical burns it will also flush out traces of the active chemical. In the case of chemical burns, try to ensure that the water is running.
2. Remove articles of clothing where the burn source is wet, such as steam or boiling water. Leave clothing burned by a direct heat source as this will probably already be sterile. Remove any rings, bracelets or watches before the affected part begins to swell.
3. Put the casualty into a position of rest. Cover the injured part with a dressing.
4. If the casualty is badly burned but conscious, give them small amounts of cold drinks at intervals.
5. Arrange for the casualty to receive medical assistance. If they are badly burned, this should be by emergency ambulance.

Under no circumstances should you apply any lotion, fluids other than water, or treatment on the burn. This includes the traditional 'butter' treatment.

Certain specific burn problems require their own considerations.

## Clothing on fire

The flames must be extinguished immediately. If you do not have water to do this with, then the flames must be smothered with a blanket, coat or anything else similar to hand. Wrap the casualty in this to put the flames out. Do not use any material that would melt on contact with heat such as nylon, as this can complicate burns by 'melting' into the skin. If your own clothing catches fire, roll on the ground to put the flames out. After these actions, the general steps mentioned above should be followed.

## Eyes burned by a chemical

The eye must be flushed out with water immediately. Open the eyelids with your fingers to ensure complete success and try to make sure that any chemicals washed out do not burn other parts of the casualty. The best way to do this is to use a lot of water in your treatment. Apply a dressing to the eye, and call emergency medical help.

## Electricity

Burns from electricity should be treated with the general steps outlined above, but after consideration of breaking any electrical contact (see p.190).

## Mouth or throat

Burns here can be very serious, especially in children, as they can cause swelling and thus obstruct breathing. The first step must be to call an ambulance. If the casualty is conscious, try to give them sips of a cool liquid such as water to alleviate the burn and thus the swelling.

# Poisoning

As modern living becomes more and more sophisticated, so do the chemicals and substances that we use to support and fuel it. The list of poisonous substances is seemingly endless, with many now in common use in the home. To traditional forms of poisoning such as fungi and snake bites must now be added liquid chemicals, medicines, cleaning materials, narcotics, toxic fumes, photographic chemicals and many, many more. Poison can follow four basic routes into the body: by breathing fumes or gases (such as the old household gas, carbon monoxide from car exhausts, or the fumes from certain burning plastics); by swallowing substances (medicines, poisonous fungi or plants, decomposing food and so on); by injection (snake bites, insect stings, deliberately taken injected drugs); and by absorption through the skin (certain agricultural pesticides, and certain chemicals such as mercury).

Whether the poison has been taken accidentally or deliberately, the steps to follow are the same:

1. Call an emergency ambulance.
2. Ask the casualty what has happened. In the case of children, do not just ask if they have taken any medicines or tablets, but ask them if they have eaten any sweets. This is because children often mistake brightly coloured tablets or capsules for sweets.
3. Try to obtain samples of the source of poisoning. This is for the hospital to analyse if necessary. For the same reason, if the casualty is sick, collect a sample of the vomit in a container or plastic bag for the ambulancemen to take with them.
4. If the casualty has lost consciousness, lie them on their chest with their head on its side.
5. If the casualty has stopped breathing, apply artificial respiration. Likewise, if their heart has stopped beating, apply external heart compression.

# Electrocution

An electric shock can cause severe or even fatal injuries. These include: stopping the casualty's breathing because of either a spasm of the respiratory muscles or paralysis of the 'breathing' part of the brain; stopping the heart from beating or making its rate irregular; causing burns that could be much deeper than they appear; and causing a general shock reaction most acute in the parts of the body that the current passes through.

In all these cases, treatment should be as normal for the injury. For instance, if breathing stops, then you must apply artificial respiration. Likewise, if the casualty has a burn, then you must treat the burn as you would any other.

But the first step in dealing with an electrocution victim is to ensure that contact has been broken. If they are still in contact with the power source and you touch them yourself then you may well be electrocuted as well. Breaking contact must therefore be your priority.

In the event of somebody being electrocuted by a high voltage such as an overhead pylon, do not attempt to break contact or even approach them. Voltages such as these will 'jump' any improvised insulation. Instead, call the police.

In the event of electrocution by a low voltage such as a domestic electricity supply, one of the following steps should be taken:

1. Switch off the faulty appliance or source of electrocution at the mains or at the wall plug. If this is not possible,
2. Wrench the cable out at either the wall or the appliance. Do not touch either the appliance or the casualty, as both might be 'live'. If this is not possible,
3. Break contact with a non-conducting instrument such as a length of wood, a loop of rope or clothing or an item of furniture.

Then and only then can you apply first aid. In the event of any serious or frightening electric shock, immediately call an ambulance.

## Unconsciousness

To both the experienced and the inexperienced first aider, unconsciousness in a casualty is one of the most difficult of all conditions to handle. One of your greatest sources of help and information has deserted you – the casualty themselves. What has happened? Are they in pain, and if so where? Are they breathing easily? The answers to all these questions you will have to assess yourself, and you yourself must take action.

Step one with an unconscious casualty is always to call an emergency ambulance. Even if the casualty is drunk and cannot be aroused, do not hesitate to dial 999. Always stay with an unconscious casualty as changes in their state will have to be spotted by you; they are not going to be able to call out to you. In general, the following steps should be taken:

1. Clear the casualty's mouth of anything that might obstruct their breathing, including false teeth. Your job is to make it as easy as possible for the casualty to breathe until the ambulance arrives.

With an unconscious casualty, clear the mouth of obstructions

2. Loosen tight clothing, especially around the neck, waist and chest.
3. Ensure that the casualty has a good air supply. For instance, if the casualty is known to have been overcome by poisonous gases, remove them from the vicinity and take them into fresh air.
4. If breathing fails or shows signs of failing, apply artificial respiration. Likewise, if the casualty is bleeding, try to control the flow.
5. If you are certain that the casualty could not have damaged their back or spine, then very carefully turn them on to their chest with their head on one side. This will allow any

blood or vomit in their throat to drain away without obstructing their breathing. If there is any chance, however, that the back or spine may have been injured, then you should avoid any unnecessary movements whatsoever, as these may compound the injury.
6. Cover the casualty with blankets or coats to keep them warm.

## Shock

Sometimes after an accident, you may notice that the casualty is feeling giddy, they are sweating, and their skin feels cold.

Shock victims should be laid in a position of rest

Perhaps they feel sick or thirsty, or unnecessarily worried. These could all be caused by shock. Shock is actually more than just fright or horror; it is a specific medical condition caused by the casualty not supplying enough blood to their vital organs. The results of shock can vary from just faintness or giddiness to serious illness or even death.

Many things can cause shock, including a loss of fluids such as blood, plasma or even recurrent vomiting, and heart attacks. In general, the following steps should be taken:

1. Call emergency medical help.
2. Lay the casualty down in a position of rest. If the injury that caused the shock is apparent, then treat that.
3. Loosen clothing, especially at the neck, chest and waist.
4. If necessary, such as at the scene of a road accident, cover the casualty with a blanket or coat to keep them warm.
5. If the casualty complains of thirst, dampen their lips with water, but avoid giving them anything to drink.

You should also avoid any 'external' heating of the casualty (such as a hot water bottle or electric fire) as this can 'draw' blood from their vital organs. You should avoid moving the casualty as well.

# USEFUL INFORMATION

## Addresses

Age Concern England
Bernard Sunley House
Pitcairn Road
Mitcham
London (01-640 5431)

Alcohol Concern
305 Grays Inn Road
London WC1X 8QF (01-833 3471)

Asbestos Information Centre Ltd
St Andrews House
22-28 High Street
Epsom
Surrey KT19 8AH (78-42055)

Asbestos Removal Contractors
    Association (ARCA)
45 Sheen Lane
London SW14 8AB (01-876 4415)

ASH-Action on Smoking and
    Health
5-11 Mortimer Street
London W1N 7RH (01-637 9843)

Association of Community Health
    Councils for England & Wales
362 Euston Road
London NW1 3BL (01-388 4814)

Asociation of British Insurers
    (ABI)
Aldermary House
Queen Street
London EC4N 1TT (01-248 4477)

Association of Optical
    Practitioners (AOP)
Bridge House
233-234 Blackfriars Road
London SE1 8NW (01-261 9661)

Automobile Association
Fanum House
Basingstoke
Hants RG21 2EA (0256 20123)

British Activity Holiday
    Association
PO Box 99
Tunbridge Wells
Kent TN1 2EL (0892 49868)

British Association of Leisure
    Parks, Piers and Attractions
    (formerly Association of
    Amusement Parks and Piers)
23 Bedford Row
London WC1R 4EB (01-405 1450)

BEAB – British Electrotechnical
  Approvals Board
Mark House
9-11 Queens Road
Hersham
Walton-on-Thames
Surrey KT12 5NA (0932 244401)

British Fire Protection Systems
  Association (BFPSA)
48A Eden Street
Kingston-upon-Thames
Surrey KT1 1EE (01-549 8839)

British Pyrotechnists Association
PO Box 31
London SW1P 4LW (01-405 4245)

British Red Cross Society
9 Grosvenor Crescent
London SW1X 7EJ (01-235 5454)

British Standards Institution (BSI)
Linford Wood
Milton Keynes MK14 6LE
  (0908 221166)

Building Research Establishment
  (BRE)
Garston
Watford
Herts WD2 7JR (0923 674040)

Chemical Industries Association
  Ltd (CIA)
Kings Buildings
Smith Square
London SW1P 3JJ

Child Accident Prevention Trust
75 Portland Place
London W1N 3AL (01-636 2545)

Committee on Safety of Medicines
Market Towers
1 Nine Elms Lane
London SW8 5NQ (01-720 2188)

Consumers' Association
2 Marylebone Road
London NW1 4DX
  (01-546 5544)

Consumer Safety Unit
Department of Trade and Industry
10-18 Victoria Street
London SW1H ONQ
  (01-215 3267)

CORGI-Confederation for the
  Registration of Gas Installers
St Martins House
140 Tottenham Court Road
London W1P 9LN (01-387 9185)

DHSS-Department of Health &
  Social Security
Alexander Fleming House
Elephant and Castle
London SE1 6BY (01-407 5522)

Design Council
28 Haymarket
London SW1Y 4SU (01-839 8000)

Fair Play for Children Charitable
  Trust/National Committee
  for the Safety of Children at Play
137 Homerton High Street
London E9

Fire Extinguising Trades
  Association (FETA)
48A Eden Street
Kingston-upon-Thames
Surrey KT1 1EE (01-549 8839)

Firework Makers' Guild
c/o 2-8 Foredown Drive
Portslade
Brighton
BN4 2BB (0273 204737)

Fire Protection Association (FPA)
140 Aldersgate Street
London EC1A 4HX (01-606 3757)

Fire Research Station (FRS)
Borehamwood
Herts WD6 2BL (01-953 6177)

Glass and Glazing Federation
  (GGF)
44-48 Borough High Street
London SE1 1XB (01-403 7177)

Health Education Authority
  (HEA-formerly Health
  Education Council)
78 New Oxford Street
London WC1A 1AH (01-631
0930)

Health and Safety Agency for
  Northern Ireland
Canada House
North Street
Belfast BT1 1NW (0232 243249)

Health and Safety Executive
  (HSE)

Public Enquiry Points:

HSE
Library and Information Services
Broad Lane
Sheffield S3 7HQ (0742 752539);

HSE
Library and Information Services
St Hughs House
Stanley Precinct
Bootle
Merseyside L20 3QY (051-951
  4381);

HSE
Library and Information Services
Baynards House
1 Chepstow Place
Westbourne Grove
London W2 4TF (01-221 0870)

Health Services Commissioner
  (Ombudsman)
Church House
Great Smith Street
London SW1P 3BW (01-212 7676)

HMSO – Her Majesty's Stationery
  Office
Publications Centre
PO Box 276
London SW8 5DT (orders 01-622
  3316; all other purposes 01-211
  5656)

(Government bookshops in:
  London; Edinburgh;
  Manchester; Bristol;
  Birmingham; Belfast)

Home Office
50 Queen Anne's Gate
London SW1H 9AT (01-213 3000)

Institute of Consumer Advisers
Flat 6
24 Rye Lane
London SE15 5BS (01-703 5049)

ITSA – Institute of Trading
   Standards Administration
Metropolitan House
Third Floor
37 Victoria Avenue
Southend-on-Sea
Essex SS2 6DA (0702 338313)

Insurance Ombudsman Bureau
31 Southampton Row
London WC1B 5HJ (01-242 8613)

Law Society
113 Chancery Lane
London WC2A 1PL (01-242 1222)

Law Society of Northern Ireland
Law Society House
90 Victoria Street
Belfast BT1 3JZ (0232 231614)

Law Society of Scotland
26-27 Drumsheugh Gardens
Edinburgh EH3 7YR (031-226
   7411)

NACAB – National Association of
Citizens Advice Bureaux
Myddleton House
115-123 Pentonville Road
London N1 9LZ (01-833 2181)

NCC – National Consumer
   Council
20 Grosvenor Gardens
London SW1W ODH (01-730
   3469)

NFCG – National Federation of
Consumer Groups
12 Mosley Street
Newcastle-upon-Tyne
NE1 1DE (091-261 8259)

NICEIC – National Inspection
   Council for Electrical
   Contracting
Vintage House
36-37 Albert Embankment
London SE1 7UJ (01-582 7746)

National Pharmaceutical
   Association
Mallinson House
40-42 St Peter's Street
St Albans
Herts AL1 3NP (0727 32161)

Northern Ireland Association of
   Citizens Advice Bureaux
New Forge Lane
Belfast BT1 5NW (0232 681118)

OFT – Office of Fair Trading
Field House
15-25 Bream's Buildings
London EC4A 1PR (01-242 2858)

OIC – Optical Information
   Council
19-24 Temple Chambers
Temple Avenue
London EC4Y ODT (01-353 3556)

RETRA – Radio Electrical &
   Television Retailers' Association
RETRA House
57-61 Newington Causeway
London SE1 6BE (01-403 1463)

Royal Institution of Chartered
  Surveyors
12 Great George Street
London SW1A 3AD (01-222 7000)

RoSPA – Royal Society for the
  Prevention of Accidents
Cannon House
Priory Queensway
Birmingham B4 6BS
  (021-200 2461)

RLSS – Royal Life Saving Society
Mountbatten House
Studley
Warwickshire B80 7NN
  (052 785 3943)

RNIB – Royal National Institute
  for the Blind
224 Great Portland Street
London W1 (01-388 1266)

St John Ambulance
1 Grosvenor Crescent
London SW1X 7EF (01-235 5231)

SCODA – Standing Conference on
  Drug Abuse
1-4 Hatton Place
London EC1N 8ND (01-430 2341)

SPAID – Society for the
  Prevention of Asbestosis and
  Industrial Diseases
38 Drapers Road
Enfield
Middlesex EN2 8LU
  (01-366 1640)

SMMT – Society of Motor
  Manufacturers & Traders
Forbes House
Halkin Street
London SW1X 7DS (01-235 7000)

Sports Council
16 Upper Woburn Place
London WC1H OQP
  (01-388 1277)

---

# Journals

Which?
Motoring Which?
Holiday Which?
– for address see Consumers' Association

Care on the Road
Care in the Home
Safety Education
RoSPA Bulletin
– for address see RoSPA

# INDEX

Entries in **bold type** refer to main sections in the text; entries in italics normally refer to officially published regulations and acts